Burbage Fallen of World War Two

The Personal Stories of those who fell in WW2

Biographies Researched and Written by Geoff Whitworth

Additional Information by Greg Drozdz

Burbage Heritage Group

Book Design and Layout by Paul Williams

Burbage Fallen of the Second World War

Copyright © (Burbage Heritage Group 2025)

No part of this book may be reproduced in any form by photocopying or any electronic or mechanical means including information storage or retrieval systems, without the permission in writing from the copyright owner and the publisher of the book.

ISBN: 9781836906636

First published in 2025 by BookVAULT Publishing, Peterborough, United Kingdom

To Greg Drozdz

Your intense interest in our local
history has been the inspiration for much of the
fallen histories and stories told in this book.
Your work has been a catalyst for further research in many areas

Acknowledgments

The Burbage Heritage Group thanks everyone who contributed to this book, especially the families of the fallen for providing records, photos, and memories.

Special thanks to Greg Drozdz for writing "Yanks for the Memory" and "Poles Apart".

We also appreciate the financial support from Burbage Parish Land Charity, which helps distribute free copies to local schools, libraries, and churches.

CONTENTS

Introduction 7
   Burbage Heritage Group 7
   Research of the WW1 & WW2 Fallen 7
   Centennial Anniversary of Death of WW1 Fallen 8
   World War Two – WW2 8
   75 Year Anniversary of the end of WW2 9
   Naming Changes 9
The Burbage War Memorial 10
   Village Memorial 10
   Memorial to WW2 Fallen 11
The Fallen 17
   Corporal James Frederick Allen 18
   Private Charles Frank Barnes 21
   Driver Stanley Clarke 23
   Driver Edward Samuel Bernard Colkin 25
   Private Dennis Comer 27
   Private Sydney Charles Comer 29
   Captain Edward Thomas Crump 32
   Sapper Victor Charles Davies 34
   Gunner Harry Dobson 37
   Able Seaman Horace Hadley 39
   Sergeant George Harrison 41
   Private Frank Holyoak 44
   Sergeant Pilot Frederick John Howarth 47
   Lance Corporal Frederick Harold Howkins 51
   Able Seaman Percy Jarvis 54
   Driver Leslie David Jones 56
   Private Richard Joseph Kearns 58
   Squadron Leader Sidney Edward Kellaway 60
   Lance Corporal Harold Letts 63
   Aircraftsman Kenneth Bert Lockton 66
   Warrant Officer John Lord 67
   Aircraftsman 1st Class Stanley Richard Lount 71
   Private Frank Moore 73
   Flight Lieutenant George William Nickerson MM 75
   Private Francis Pritchard 79
   Mr Sydney Harry Shaw 81
   Sergeant George Henry Smith 83
   Lieutenant Thomas Frank Smith 87
   Trooper Bert Edward Thatcher 89
   Gunner Jeffrey Tite 92

- Fusilier Walter White ... 94
- Corporal Douglas Arthur Wood ... 96

Thailand – Burma Railway ... 100
- Dobson & Tite's Journey to the Far East ... 100
- Surrender of Singapore and transfer to Thailand ... 101
- Private Dobson, Corporal Letts and Private Tite ... 102
- Memorial to those who died ... 102

Military Deaths In Burbage ... 103
- Wellington Bomber MF-116 ... 103
- Wellington Bomber X9953 ... 108

Yanks For The Memory ... 109
- So, what was heaven like? ... 109

Poles Apart ... 114

Churches, Chapels And Other Memorials ... 116
- St Catherine's Parish Church ... 116
- Wesleyan Chapel ... 117
- Congregational Chapel ... 118
- St Peter's Roman Catholic Church, Hinckley ... 119
- Hinckley Grammar School ... 120
- Burbage Liberal Club ... 121
- Regent Club Hinckley ... 123

Burbage At War ... 124
- War is Declared ... 124
- Burbage Firemen ... 124
- Land Girls ... 124
- Blackouts ... 125
- Hinckley & Burbage Houses Bombed ... 126
- The Barracks ... 128
- Home Guard ... 129
- Co-op Hall ... 130
- Burbage Spitfire ... 131
- Dam Buster - Geoff Rice ... 131

Peace ... 133
- Victory in Europe May 1945 ... 133
- Victory in Japan August 1945 ... 134

80 Years On ... 136

Index ... 138

INTRODUCTION

Burbage Heritage Group

Burbage Heritage Group is a community-led organisation dedicated to preserving, promoting, and sharing the rich history of Burbage. Established in 2000, the group has spent the past 25 years uncovering and protecting the village's heritage, ensuring that its history is recorded and accessible for future generations. As it celebrates its 25th anniversary, the group continues to engage with the local community through a wide range of activities, fostering a deep appreciation of Burbage's past. In recognition of its outstanding contributions, Burbage Heritage Group was awarded Heritage Group of the Year in 2021 by the Leicestershire & Rutland Heritage Forum, a prestigious accolade that highlights its dedication to historical preservation and community engagement.

The group's primary aim is to safeguard the historical identity of Burbage by researching, documenting, and archiving significant events, places, and people connected to the village. Through exhibitions, guest speaker events, guided heritage walks, and publications, Burbage Heritage Group brings history to life, encouraging residents to explore and connect with their heritage.

To achieve this aim, the group has set several key objectives. One of the most important is to conserve and promote awareness of historic sites within Burbage, ensuring they are protected and appreciated. The group also collaborates with local schools and educational institutions to enhance history education, offering resources and activities that make local history engaging for younger generations. By working with teachers and students, the group fosters a love of history and ensures that future generations remain connected to Burbage's past.

Another key objective is to collect and preserve oral histories from long-time residents. These personal stories and memories provide invaluable insights into Burbage's social history, capturing details that may not be recorded in official documents. This initiative has resulted in a growing archive of personal recollections, photographs, and artifacts that help bring the village's history to life.

Figure 1 Heritage Group of the Year 2021

Additionally, the group works with local authorities, historical societies, and conservation groups to advocate for the protection of heritage buildings and landmarks. Whether through restoration projects, historical research, or awareness campaigns, the group ensures that Burbage's historic character is maintained amidst modern developments.

Burbage Heritage Group also fosters a sense of pride and belonging among residents by celebrating the village's unique identity. Through heritage events, re-enactments, and exhibitions, the group highlights Burbage's role in regional and national history, encouraging both long-standing and new residents to connect with the past. Special anniversary events and commemorations allow the community to reflect on and celebrate its rich history together.

Research of the WW1 & WW2 Fallen

The village war memorial was at the centre of the research undertaken. On the front face of the memorial are the names of fifty-four men who are commemorated, having lost their lives for their Country. Additional to these men a further six were commemorated shortly after the memorial was unveiled, having not been originally listed. Sixty men and their families were the subject of local research and investigation. Descendants, many still living in the village, came forward with stories and photographs. Other men needed much further research in the local newspaper "The Hinckley Times". We are fortunate that an archive of the paper was able to be painstakingly reviewed, to extract further stories and newspaper images. From this research biographies were prepared for each of the fallen, which sadly included the date and location of their death.

It was quickly established that whilst the research focussed upon the histories of the sixty fallen, questions were raised from the community as to those village men and boys who did not appear on this list. This prompted further research into these names which had been brought forward.

The work established that some of these additional names were actually included on other local memorials such as that at Hinckley, although it was also established that some were not listed on any public memorial. Yet more work, including a public engagement, concluded that almost 100 years on it was appropriate to add a further four names to the memorial.

The research is captured in the biographies of the 64 Burbage fallen which are documented in an earlier book *Burbage Fallen of the Great War*.

Centennial Anniversary of Death of WW1 Fallen

The engagement of schools led to simple ceremonies at the war memorial on the centennial anniversary of each soldier's death. Representative children from each of the three primary schools in the village were invited to the ceremony and the assembled group would be given a brief history of the soldier, where they lived, worked and subsequently died. The talk would expand on their families and the children were encouraged to reflect upon the sadness which would be experienced by those left behind. Descendants of the soldiers would also attend to pay their respects. On a few occasions the children also included descendants of the fallen soldier. At the end of the brief talk a candle was lit for each soldier, in all sixty-four candles were lit, during the period September 2014 until November 2018.

The group received a "Highly Commended" accolade for an entry to heritage awards, which detailed the work carried out in recognition of the 100 years since the Great War. This was a culmination of many years' research engaging the whole community in the understanding of village life and sacrifices made during the WW1 years, 1914-19. Displays, musical events, guided walks, a new memorial rose garden, craft and re-enactment events for local schools were some of the events provided.

World War Two – WW2

The Second World War (1939–1945) was one of the most significant and devastating conflicts in human history. It involved the vast majority of the world's nations, forming two opposing military alliances: the Allies and the Axis. The war was rooted in the political, economic, and social turmoil that followed the First World War, particularly the harsh terms of the Treaty of Versailles (1919), which imposed severe reparations and territorial losses on Germany. The rise of totalitarian regimes in Germany, Italy, and Japan, combined with aggressive expansionist policies, set the stage for a global conflict.

The war officially began on 1st September 1939, when Nazi Germany, under the leadership of Adolf Hitler, invaded Poland. This act prompted Britain and France to declare war on Germany two days later. The German military employed a new strategy known as Blitzkrieg ("lightning war"), which combined rapid, coordinated attacks by tanks, aircraft, and infantry, leading to the swift occupation of Poland. By mid-1940, Germany had conquered much of Western Europe, including France, Belgium, and the Netherlands. The fall of France left Britain as the primary resistance to Nazi aggression in Western Europe.

The Battle of Britain (1940) was a pivotal moment in the early phase of the war. The German Luftwaffe conducted a massive bombing campaign against Britain, aiming to destroy the Royal Air Force (RAF) and force the British government to negotiate peace. However, the RAF's resilience and effective use of radar technology enabled Britain to repel the German assault, marking Hitler's first major defeat.

In June 1941, Germany launched Operation Barbarossa, a massive invasion of the Soviet Union. Despite early successes, the German advance stalled due to fierce Soviet resistance, logistical challenges, and the harsh Russian winter. The conflict on the Eastern Front became the largest and bloodiest theatre of the war, with battles such as Stalingrad (1942–1943) and Kursk (1943) marking significant turning points in favour of the Soviet Union.

The war expanded further with Japan's attack on Pearl Harbour on 7th December 1941, which brought the United States into the conflict. Japan had already been expanding its influence across the Pacific and East Asia, including the occupation of Manchuria (1931) and the invasion of China (1937). The American entry into the war significantly bolstered the Allied position both in Europe and the Pacific.

The tide of the war began to turn decisively in 1942 and 1943. The Allies achieved major victories in North Africa (e.g., the Battle of El Alamein), the Pacific (e.g., the Battle of Midway), and on the Eastern Front (e.g., Stalingrad). In June 1944, the Allies launched Operation Overlord, commonly known as D-Day, when Allied forces landed on the beaches of Normandy in German-occupied France. This successful invasion marked the beginning of the liberation of Western Europe.

By May 1945, Allied forces had pushed into Germany, and Hitler committed suicide in his Berlin bunker. Germany surrendered on 8th May 1945 (VE Day). The war in the Pacific continued until August 1945, when the United States dropped atomic bombs on the Japanese cities of Hiroshima and Nagasaki. Japan surrendered on 2nd September 1945, bringing the war to a conclusion. The Second World War resulted in an estimated 70–85 million deaths, making it the deadliest conflict in human history.

As summarised above, WW2 was a global conflict in which 32 Burbage men are commemorated on the village Memorial, having lost their lives. Many were killed in European battles in Italy, France, the Netherlands, Austria and Germany. Others lie further afield in graves in North Africa, Thailand, Burma and India. Some died in terrible conditions as POWs of the Japanese and Germans, and others fell in fierce battles as the Allies fought their way across North Africa, Europe and the Far East. Closer to home, men lost their lives from the effects of war, and others while being trained for the conflict to come.

This book pays tribute to those who fell. Many were little more than boys, others were husbands and fathers and every death was a loss to a Burbage family. We remember them and their sacrifice.

75 Year Anniversary of the end of WW2

Building on their research for WW1, the Heritage Group extended their work to include the fallen soldiers of WW2. This comprehensive commemoration was planned for May 2020.

Despite significant progress, the Coronavirus pandemic struck at the end of 2019, leading to global lockdowns and the suspension of public gatherings.

Between 2019 and November 2020, local schools selected groups of pupils to visit the memorial in commemoration of the 75th anniversary of the soldiers' deaths. Each group was informed about the specific soldier or soldiers being remembered, with detailed biographies provided as outlined in this book.

These visits were inspired by those commemorating WW1 casualties. The aim is for children to remember their war memorial visits and continue honouring these brave men throughout their lives.

Figure 2 School visit to Burbage War Memorial 6th March 2020

Naming Changes

This book reflects on the events between 1939 and 1945, the impacts on families and the village community.

Over the 80 years which have elapsed, there have been many changes which have occurred across the world as we know it today. In this book we will attempt to make reference to countries as they were known at the time of the conflict which we now refer to as WW2. In this way we will be consistent in naming conventions within the book and the associated newspaper clipping from that time. To aid the reader we have listed some of the changes which have occurred over this period in the theatres of war which are described. For more details see page 136.

THE BURBAGE WAR MEMORIAL

Figure 3 The Burbage War Memorial 2021

Village Memorial

Along with many other villages across the country, as the 'Great War' came to a formal end in July 1919, Burbage families were planning a recognition of those men who had lost their lives in the service of their country. A committee was formed in the village to oversee the arrangement for the erection of a fine marble memorial. Although there was originally disagreement about the location of the memorial, in 1921 a marble memorial was unveiled on the village green. A local newspaper report records *"The memorial is a strikingly beautiful one, and consists of a massive pedestal, placed on a heavy base of Bishopgate stone, and surmounted by a life-size figure of a British Tommy, with arms reversed, cut in Carrara Marble. A more exquisite piece of work is probably not found in the whole of Leicestershire"*

Figure 4 1921 unveiling of the Burbage War Memorial

Around the memorial was laid a rose garden with a named rose dedicated to each of the fallen. The garden was surrounded by a holly hedge at the triangular plot. The memorial is situated in the centre of the village in Church Street.

Figure 5 War Memorial c1939

Memorial to WW2 Fallen

The photograph above taken from behind in the late 1930s shows the rear, north, blank face of the memorial. It is this face which would have the names of the fallen in WW2 added in 1948.

A public meeting was held in the Co-operative Hall, which was immediately across the road from the War Memorial to the Fallen of WW1, on Tuesday 11th February 1947. The purpose of the meeting was to "*Receive suggestions as to what form the war memorial [to WW2 fallen] shall take.*"

The meeting was chaired by Cllr T McGrah. At the meeting one of the suggestions made was that the Rectory, which was about to come onto the market, could provide a nucleus for a memorial for the village fallen.

A number of interesting suggestions were put forward including; the provision of a maternity home, the laying out of a part of the village as a memorial garden where people could find rest and seclusion amid pleasant surroundings, and a building where youth could find recreation away from the licensed premises.

However, the provision of a village hall lost favour with the meeting because of the long time that would of necessity elapse before the scheme could be completed.

The meeting was unanimous that Burbage should have a memorial quite apart from the one contemplated by Hinckley and they favoured a suggestion from Mr J Petcher that a plaque, bearing the names of the fallen of 'The Second Great War' be added to the existing memorial.

The following were appointed as a committee with power to co-opt:

Mr A Chamberlain	Mr John Iliffe
Mrs A Chamberlain	Mr S R Millar
Mr H Collins	Mr J Petcher
Mr J T Evans	Mr E Robinson
Mr J Handley Junr	Mrs S E Kellaway

Mr Chamberlain acted as secretary for the meeting and Burbage councillors of Hinckley Urban District Council would be ex-officio members of the committee.

The committee met on Thursday 6th March 1947 with Cllr McGrah again in the chair. Representatives from all of the leading village organisations had been invited and there were lively discussions on the various proposals which had been brought forward. A report was presented from the County Council which concluded that it would be 'useless' to proceed with the proposal for a maternity home at Burbage and with regret the meeting agreed to abandon the idea.

With regard to the idea of a memorial garden it was suggested there were many difficulties with the plan. It was agreed to defer the decision until a further public meeting planned for the 8th May 1947. The committee also decided to invite the next of kin of the fallen to be present at the following meeting. At that meeting it would be decided whether anything further was required other than a new plaque to the existing memorial and replacing the holly hedge with a stone wall and a 'good type' of gate.

At the public meeting of the 8th May it was agreed that only the additional plaque and the replacement of the holly hedge would be taken forward, although some members of the meeting expressed a preference to retain the holly hedge. It was decided that the secretary would seek expert advice as to the most suitable type of wall which would blend with the existing memorial and obtain quotations for the work. A further public meeting would be planned for no later than August 1947 to consider the committee's recommendations.

Newspaper reports in December 1947 detail that a meeting was held to review the estimates for the work. The meeting heard that the costs for the inscriptions, wall and gate would be £557. The meeting concluded that this sum of money was unlikely to be raised and that it was resolved to limit the works to inscribing the names on the north side of the existing memorial.

In February 1948 the secretary of the committee wrote to the relatives of the fallen asking that they send him the names and particulars of their loved ones, in order that they could be inscribed.

Earlier in the year, it was decided that more funds were needed. In April 1948, the committee organised a house-to-house collection. The British Legion Women's section helped by delivering and collecting envelopes, to each door in the village, to raise the money necessary to add inscriptions to the original memorial.

Public Notices

BURBAGE MEMORIAL TO THE FALLEN

RELATIVES of those who died, both forces and civilians, at the Call of Duty, 1939-1945, are asked to send their full names and particulars to the address below on or before March 20th, 1948, in order that their names may be inserted on the existing Memorial.
J. H. ILIFFE, Esq., Hon. Sec.
113, Sapcote Road,
Burbage, Leics.
Tel No. Burbage 232   5454

Figure 6 Hinckley Times 9th April 1948

BURBAGE WAR MEMORIAL COMMITTEE

HOUSE-TO-HOUSE COLLECTION
at **Burbage**
WEEK COMMENCING APRIL 12
You are asked to honour the dead by subscribing towards the cost of inscribing on the existing memorial the names of the men of Burbage who died where duty called 1939-45. Envelopes will be delivered and called for by members of the British Legion Women's Section during the week.

Figure 7 Hinckley Times 9th April 1948

The committee held a further public meeting at the Grove Road School on Friday 24th September 1948 to announce and finalise their plans for the unveiling of the names on the memorial.

The committee arranged for the new names to be unveiled on Sunday 24th October 1948. The service held at the war memorial was led by The Reverend Richard Pughe and the guest invited to unveil the names was The Right Honourable Lord Cromwell.

Lord Cromwell, Robert Godfrey Wolsley Bewicke-Copley, 5th Baron Cromwell would have been a well-known local choice. Previously a Colonel in the army, he fought in both World Wars, becoming captured as a prisoner of war on the fall of France in 1940. He was the holder of the Distinguished Service Order and the Military Cross. Lord Cromwell resided at Misterton Hall near Lutterworth for many years, where he bred Angus Cattle. In 1946 he was elected as Hon. National Treasurer of the British Legion. Less than a year after the unveiling ceremony in Burbage he was appointed Lord-Lieutenant of Leicestershire, a role he would fulfil until 1965.

A report in the Hinckley Times records that the unveiling was carried out 'on a beautiful autumn afternoon'. A large gathering of villagers attended the ceremony.

The unveiling revealed a list of 31 men who gave their lives, including one who was killed during an air raid on Coventry. Burbage Rector, The Rev. Richard Pughe dedicated the memorial and The Rev. G E Pinfield led the prayers. Mr P J Thompson read the scriptures. Other notable dignitaries were County Councillor Mr R H Simmonds, District Councillor T. McGrah, Mrs T Flavell, Mr John Iliffe (Secretary of the Committee) and Mr J Petcher (Treasurer of the Committee and Chairman of Burbage Branch of the British Legion).

The Destiny of the Righteous

But the souls of the righteous are in the hand of God,
and no torment will ever touch them.
In the eyes of the foolish they seemed to have died,
and their departure was thought to be a disaster,
and their going from us to be their destruction;
but they are at peace.
For though in the sight of others they were punished,
their hope is full of immortality.
Having been disciplined a little, they will receive great good,
because God tested them and found them worthy of himself;
like gold in the furnace he tried them,
and like a sacrificial burnt-offering he accepted them.
In the time of their visitation they will shine forth,
and will run like sparks through the stubble.
They will govern nations and rule over peoples,
and the Lord will reign over them for ever.
Those who trust in him will understand truth,
and the faithful will abide with him in love,
because grace and mercy are upon his holy ones,
and he watches over his elect.

Wisdom of Solomen 3:1-9

Immediately before the unveiling Mr Thompson read the scripture 'Wisdom of Solomen 3:1-9. Having unveiled the names Lord Cromwell gave a short address in which he said;

> *"The Legion's act of homage should not be mere idle words but something with a real meaning that must exist for ever. Though there was no longer any glory in war that did not mean there was any less glory of those who made the supreme sacrifice. Without dwelling on the uncertain and difficult times which confronted us again, it behoved everyone to keep his candles lit and his armour bright, and so win the peace which everyone of them desired and for which their menfolk died."*

The committee published their final accounts in December of 1948. The accounts disclosed that the memorial works and unveiling ceremony in total cost £100 5s 6d. with £81 6s being collected via the house-to-house collection carried out by the British Legion, the remaining funds being provided by Hinckley Urban District Council and special subscriptions.

BURBAGE WAR MEMORIAL COMMITTEE.

113 Sapcote Road,
BURBAGE,
Leics.

Mrs. S. Kellaway,
Wolvey Road,
Burbage.

13th October, 1948.

Dear Mrs. Kellaway,

On Sunday afternoon October 24th 1948. your late Husband's name will be honoured and commemorated by the people of Burbage. The Rt. Hon. Lord Cromwell, D.S.O. M.C. D.L. J.P., Chairman of the British Legion of Great Britain, has very kindly consented to be present to perform the unveiling ceremony of the newly inscribed names on the Memorial of all those men of Burbage who made the "Supreme Sacrifice".

A special place has been reserved for you at the Memorial Service and the War Memorial Committee give you this personal invitation to be present.

The ceremony commences at 3 o'clock, but it is asked that you be there at 2.45 in order that you may take up your rightful place at the Memorial. A special table is being provided on which flowers and wreaths may be placed before the ceremony commences. Afterwards, these may be placed on the Memorial by yourself if you so wish.

I am enclosing a specially printed souvenir card giving the form of the unveiling service, which we trust will be some small token which you may desire to keep in honour of your late Husband's memory.

Yours very sincerely,

Hon. Secretary.

Figure 8 Letter Inviting Mrs Kellaway to the Unveiling Ceremony

War Memorial Unveiled At Burbage

On a beautiful autumn afternoon and in the presence of a large gathering of villagers. Burbage's memorial to those who gave their lives. In World War II, was, on Sunday unveiled by Lord Cromwell D.S.O., M.C., D.L., J.P.

The memorial takes the form of an addition to the one erected in honour of the men of the 1914/18 War, and bears the names of 31 men of the village who gave their lives, including one who was killed during a raid on Coventry.

Supporting Lord Cromwell was the Rector, Rev. R.D.H. Pughe who dedicated the memorial, Rev. G.E. Pinfield who led the prayers, Mr. P.J. Thompson who read the scriptures, Mr. R.H. Simmons C.C., Mrs. T. Flavel, Councillor T. McGrah, Messrs. John Iliffe (secretary), and Mr. J. Pletcher (treasurer).

The British Legion paraded to the service, the Burbage Silver Prize Band led the singing of the hymns, and Mr. J. Pletcher recited the British Legion's Act of Homage.

"NO GLORY IN WAR"

Having performed the unveiling ceremony. Lord Cromwell gave a short address in which he said the Legion's Act of homage should not be mere idea words but something with a real meaning that must exist for ever. Though there was no longer any glory in war that did not mean there was any less glory of those who made the supreme sacrifice. Without dwelling on the uncertain and difficult times which confronted us again, it behoved everyone to keep his candles lit and his armour bright, and so win the peace which everyone of them desired and for which their menfolk died.

The hymns "O God Our help in Ages past" and "O Valiant Hearts" were sung, and the Last Post and Reveille sounded.

THE FALLEN

The names of the men inscribed on the memorial are: Pte. J. Allen, Northants Regt. ; Pts. C. F. Barnes, 1st Leicester Regt. ; Drv. S. Clarke, R.A.S.C. ;Drv. E.S.B. Colkin, R.A.S.C. ; Pte. S.C. Comer, 6th Leicester Regt. ; Pte. D. S. Comer, Northants Regt. Captain E.T. Crump, R.E.; Spr. V.C. Davies R.E. ; Gnr. H. Dobson R.A. ; A/B H. Hadley ; Sgt. G. Harrison, 7th Leicester Regt. Pte. F. Holyoak, 5th Leicester Rgt.; Sgt. Pilot F. J. Howarth R.A.F.V.R.; Lance Corpl. F.H. Howkins, 8th Leicester Regt. ; A/B P. Jarvis ; Drv. L.D. Jones, R.A.S.C. ; Sqdr. Ldr. S.E. Kellaway, R.A.F. ; Pte. R.J. Kearns, Queen's Royal Regt. ; Lance Corpl. H. Letts, - 1st Leicester Regt. ; A.C.1 K.B. Lockton, R.A.F. ; Warrant Officer J. Lord, R.A.F. ; A.C.1 S.R. Lount, R.A.S.C. ; Pte. F. Moore, 2nd Forresters ; F/lt G.W. Nickerson, M.M. R.A.F. ; Pte. F. Pritchard, 14th Sherwood Forresters ; S.H. Shaw, N.F.S. ; Lt. T.F. Smith, R.A. ; Tpr. B.E. Thatcher, 4th Hussars ; Gnr. J. Tite, R.A. ; Fus. W. White, Royal Irish ; Cpl. D.A. Wood, 1st Northants Regt. The memorial scheme was evolved and carried through by a committee of villagers, wholeheartedly supported by members of the British Legion, and the cost of frayed by public subscription.

The inscriptions and work on the memorial was carried out by Mr. George Williams, of Mount Road, Hinckley.

Figure 9 1948 Unveiling ceremony programme

Figure 10 Rt. Hon. Lord Cromwell, D.S.O., M.C., D.L., J.P.

Left: Figure 11 Hinckley Times 29 October 1948

IN HONOURED MEMORY OF
THE MEN OF BURBAGE
WHO DIED WHERE DUTY CALLED
1939 – 1945.

CPL. J. ALLEN NORTHANTS REGT.
PTE. C. F. BARNES 1/LEICS. REGT.
DRV. S. CLARKE R.A.S.C.
DRV. E. S. B. COLKIN R.A.S.C.
PTE. S. C. COMER 6/LEICS. REGT.
CAPT. E. T. CRUMP R.E.
PTE. D. S. COMER 5/NORTHANTS REGT.
SPR. V. C. DAVIES R.E.
CUNR. H. DOBSON R.A.
SGT. C. HARRISON 7/LEICS. REGT.
PTE. F. HOLYOAK 5/LEICS. REGT.
SGT. PILOT. F. J. HOWARTH R.A.F.V.R.
L/CPL. F. H. HOWKINS 8/LEICS. REGT.
A/B. P. JARVIS.
DRV. L. D. JONES R.A.S.C.
SQDR/LDR. S. E. KELLAWAY R.A.F.
L/CPL. H. LETTS 1/LEICS. REGT.
A.C.I. K. B. LOCKTON R.A.F.
WARRANT OFFICER. J. LORD R.A.F.
A.C.I. S. M. LOUNT R.A.F.
PTE. F. MOORE 2/FORRESTERS.
F/LT. C. W. NICKERSON M.M. R.A.F.
PTE. F. PRITCHARD 14TH SHERWOOD FORRESTERS.
S. H. SHAW N.F.S.
LT. T. F. SMITH R.A.
TR. B. E. THATCHER IV/HUSSARS.
CUNR. J. TITE R.A.
FUS. W. WHITE R. IRISH.
CPL. D. A. WOOD 1/NORTHANTS REGT.
A/B. H. HADLEY.
PTE. R. J. KEARNS QUEEN'S ROYAL REGT.
SGT. G. H. SMITH 2/ROYAL BERKS. REGT.

Previous Page: Figure 12 Burbage War Memorial North Face

The Fallen

The biographies of those men commemorated on Burbage War Memorial

CORPORAL JAMES FREDERICK ALLEN

Service Number: 5889196
Enlisted: 2nd Battalion Northamptonshire Regiment
Born: 24th March 1920, Smockington
Died: Wednesday 24th May 1944, Aged 24
Memorials: Beach Head War Cemetery, Anzio, Italy
Plot XV, Row B, Grave 9
Burbage St Catherine's Church Memorial
Burbage War Memorial

James, known to his family as Jim, was the youngest son of Tom and Emily Allen. His father worked for the Cooperative Farm that owned much of the land in the Wolvey area. The family lived in a tied cottage at Smockington on the A5, Watling Street. It was here that Jim was born and grew up with his brothers and sisters. Across the fields was the village of Wolvey where Jim attended the small village school.

Figure 13 A5 Watling Street

On leaving school, he was employed by the Hinckley Urban District Council in the Highways Department as a General Labourer working on road maintenance.

In 1940, Jim joined the army and was posted to the Northamptonshire Regiment. He married Frances, a girl from Nuneaton and moved to 14 Strutt Road, Burbage.

After various postings, Jim returned home in the summer of 1943 to spend some time with his wife and new baby daughter Barbara. In the autumn, Jim was posted overseas and his wife returned to live near her family in Nuneaton.

On 3rd September 1943, the Allies invaded the Italian mainland, the invasion coinciding with an armistice with the Italians who then re-entered the war on the Allied side. It was about this time that Jim and his regiment, 2nd Battalion Northampton Regiment were posted overseas.

Progress of the Allied troops was rapid, but by the end of October, the Allies faced the German winter defensive known as the Gustav Line, which stretched from the river Garigliano in the West to the Sangro in the East. Initial attempts were unsuccessful and in January 1944, troops landed behind the German lines at Anzio but a breakthrough was not achieved until May. It was here under the fierce fighting that Jim was killed on Wednesday 24th May 1944; he was just 24 years of age.

Figure 14 Tied Cottages, Smockington

Jim's grave is at the Beach Head War Cemetery at Anzio, see Figure 17. The site of the cemetery originally lay close to a casualty clearing station. Burials were made directly from the battlefield after the landings at Anzio, and later after the Army moved forward; many graves were brought in from the surrounding countryside.

After the war, the cemetery was laid out. His wife chose the inscription on his commonwealth war grave:

> **Roses May Wither**
> **Leaves May die**
> **Friends will forget you**
> **But never will I**

Many of the Allen Family have visited Anzio over the years, and his daughter is the proud owner of her father's medals, which include the Italian Star.

THE FALLEN

Figure 15 Jim Allen's wedding to his wife Frances

Figure 16 Jim with some of his comrades

Figure 17 Beach Head War Cemetery Anzio

Burbage Corporal Killed in Action

Corporal J. Allen

Cpl. Jim Allen, whose wife and baby daughter live at 67, Earls Road, Nuneaton, has been reported killed in action with the Central Mediterranean Forces.

Cpl. Allen, who was 24, was the youngest son of Mr. and Mrs. T. Allen, of Smockington, and before joining the Army four years ago resided in Lutterworth Road, Burbage. He was an employee of the Hinckley Urban District Council. Cpl. Allen left this country for overseas service about eight months ago.

Much sympathy is felt for his young wife and his parents in their bereavement.

Figure 18 Hinckley Times 30th June 1944

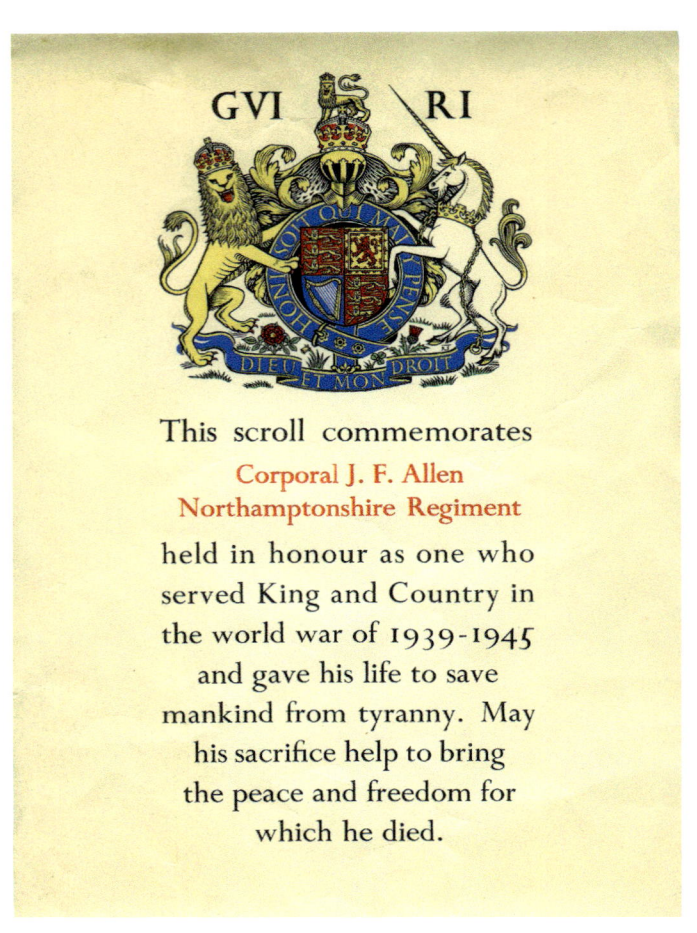

Figure 19 James F Allen, Citations and Medals

PRIVATE CHARLES FRANK BARNES

Service Number: 4868069

Enlisted: Leicestershire Regiment

Born: 1923

Died: 13th August 1944, Aged 21

Memorials: La Delivrande War Cemetery, Calvados, France, Plot 3, Row B, Grave 10

Congregational Church Memorial

St Catherine's Church Memorial

Burbage War Memorial

Charles Frank Barnes was born in 1923, the first child of Walter and Mary Ann Barnes (née Towers) of 22 Woodland Avenue, Burbage.

Before enlisting with the Leicestershire Regiment, Charles was employed at H Flude & Co. of Rugby Road, Hinckley.

Charles, who was 21, had been in the army for nearly three years. He was serving in the infantry regiment and went to France two weeks after D Day.

According to a report in the Hinckley Times of 1st September 1944, his parents were informed that Charles had been grievously wounded and was in hospital, a further communication confirmed that he had died.

Pte. C. F. Barnes

A few days after Mr. and Mrs. Walter Barnes, of 22, Woodland Avenue, Burbage, had received news that their eldest son, Pte. Charles Frank Barnes, had been wounded in the fighting in France and that he was dangerously ill in hospital, they received a further communication to say that he had died from wounds.

Pte. Barnes, who was 21, had been in the Army nearly three years. He was serving in an infantry regiment and went to France a fortnight after D-Day.

Before joining up Pte. Barnes was employed at H. Flude and Co., Rugby Road, Hinckley.

Much sympathy is felt for the parents in their bereavement.

Figure 20 Hinckley Times Report

The Allied offensive in north-western Europe began with the Normandy landings on 6 June 1944. Burials in La Delivrande War Cemetery mainly date from that day and the Sword Beach landings, especially Oboe and Peter sectors. The bodies of those killed in action in the battlefields between the coast and Caen, were later moved to this cemetery. There are 942 Commonwealth servicemen of the Second World War buried or commemorated in this cemetery. The cemetery also contains 193 German graves.

Figure 21 Pte C F Barnes Grave, La Delivrande

Barnes Family Story

John and Ellen Barnes from Northamptonshire, were Charles' Grandparents. The couple had twelve children, the last three being born in Burbage. Sadly the eldest two daugthers would die as young women, and John & Ellen saw five of their sons go off to war in WW1. Another son would die from TB at the age of 17 years.

Three sons would return from WW1, one, Arthur, was awarded the Miltary Medal. Sadly two sons, Charles and Frank died in the conflict. Their stories are told in 'Burbage Fallen of the Great War'. John and Ellen's second son Walter married Mary Ann Towers. Walter and Mary Ann named their first son - Charles Frank Barnes, his story is told here.

Walter's brothers Charles and Frank and his son Charles Frank are all remembered on the Burbage War Memorial.

Figure 22 La Delivrande War Cemetery, Calvados, France

Figure 23 Graves Registration Report

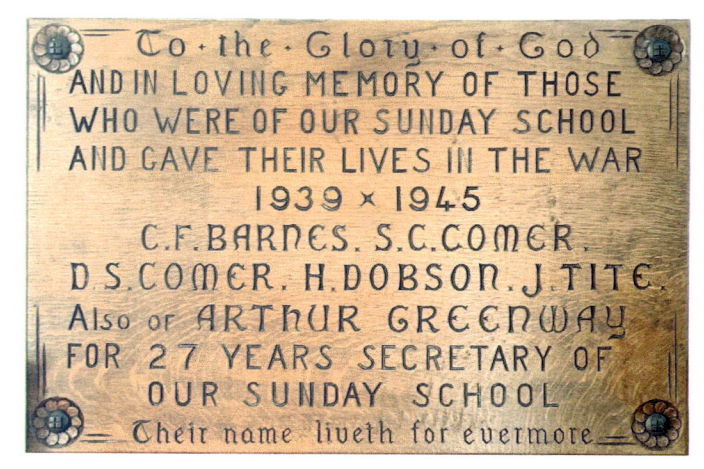

Figure 24 Congregational Church Memorial

DRIVER STANLEY CLARKE

Service Number: T/211260
Enlisted: 310th Armoured Brigade Company, Royal Army Service Corps
Born: 22nd November 1910
Died: 20th September 1944, Aged 33
Memorials: Groesbeek Memorial, Canadian War Cemetery, Gelderland, Netherlands, Panel 9
St Catherine's Church Memorial
Burbage War Memorial

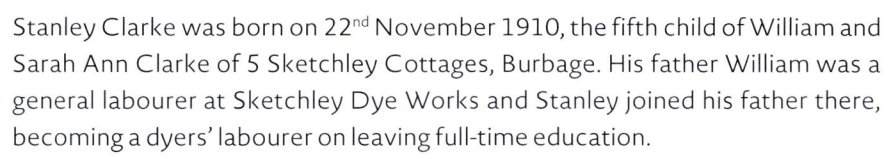

Stanley Clarke was born on 22nd November 1910, the fifth child of William and Sarah Ann Clarke of 5 Sketchley Cottages, Burbage. His father William was a general labourer at Sketchley Dye Works and Stanley joined his father there, becoming a dyers' labourer on leaving full-time education.

Stanley died 20th September 1944, aged 33, whilst serving with the 310th Armoured Brigade close to the Netherlands/German frontier. Stanley is commemorated at the Groesbeek Memorial within the Canadian War Cemetery at Gelderland, Netherlands.

Allied forces entered the Netherlands on 12th September 1944. Airborne operations later that month established a bridgehead at Nijmegen and in the following months, coastal areas and ports were cleared and secured, but it was not until the German initiated offensive in the Ardennes had been repulsed that the drive into Germany could begin.

Most of those buried in Groesbeek Canadian War Cemetery were Canadians, many of whom died in the Battle of the Rhineland. Others buried here died in the southern part of the Netherlands and the Rhineland. Within the cemetery stands Groesbeek Memorial which commemorates by name more than 1000 members of the commonwealth land forces who died during the campaign in North West Europe between the time of crossing the Seine at the end of August 1944 and the end of the war in Europe, and whose graves are unknown.

DRIVER S. CLARKE WOUNDED

Driver S. Clarke

Driver Stanley Clarke, youngest son of Mrs. Clarke and the late Mr William Clarke, of 5, Sketchley Cottages, Hinckley, has been wounded in North-West Europe. Dvr. Clarke has been in the Army four years and before being sent to France soon after D-Day, he had seen service in Iceland. He is 33 and before joining the Army was employed at Sketchley Dye Works. In pre-war days he was a member of the committee of Hinckley Angling Society.

Figure 25 Hinckley Times 27th September 1944

Left: Figure 26 Groesbeek Memorial Panel 9

Figure 27 Sketchley Dye Works 1950's, now a housing estate

Figure 28 Groesbeek Memorial

DRIVER EDWARD SAMUEL BERNARD COLKIN

Service Number: T/138311
Enlisted: 3rd Ambulance Car Company, Royal Army Service Corps
Born: 14th February 1918
Died: 24th October 1940, aged 22 whilst held prisoner of war in Germany
Memorials: Malbork Commonwealth War Cemetery, Poland, Plot 5, Row A, Grave 3.
St Catherine's Church War Memorial.
Burbage War Memorial.

Edward Samuel Bernard Colkin was born on Valentine's Day, 14th February 1918 at Church Street, Burbage, the son of Samuel and Kate Elizabeth Colkin. Bernard as he was known by his family had two elder sisters, Gladys and Freda, who were also born in the village. His father Samuel Colkin was a hosiery hand and later he was employed as a warehouse man.

The family lived at 84 Hinckley Road, by 1914 they were living at Canning House on Church Street, which may have been where Bernard was born. Canning House is the Burbage Constitutional Club, founded in 1911.

On 11th September 1922, Bernard started school in the mixed infants' class at Burbage National School under the headship of Stanley Higham. On the school photograph of Miss Dudley's Class in 1927, the nine-year-old Bernard is pictured with two other pupils, John Lord and Fredrick Howarth who also died in the War. Bernard would have been one of the first pupils at the newly opened Burbage Secondary School, in Grove Road. He left school in 1932 at the age of 14.

One of many school photographs which seemed to have been taken quite frequently in the 1920's. This particular one, chosen from many, was taken at the Church of England School in 1927, and shows (left to right) —
Back Row : Miss Dudley (Teacher), Harry Powers, Donald Gent, Jim Robins , Harold Robinson, Ray Whitmore, John Lord, Jack Briggs, Wally Smith, Stanley Meadows, Frank Reece, Bernard Colkin, Jack Simpson.
2nd Row: Myrtle Wright, Madge Spinks, Joan Scattergood, Ivy Reynolds, Alice Bass, Gwen Herbert, Mag Shilton, Nelly Shilton, Mabel Bennett, Edna Harding, Alice Cooper, Mary Craythorne, Alice Moore.
3rd Row: Ivy Bates, Mona Wright, Edna Howkins, ? , Nancy Goodwin, Eilene Robinson, Winnie Harding, Nelly Jordan, Peggy Clift, May Puffer, Eadith Beecher.
Front Row: Arthur Higginson, Fred Howarth, Jack Middleton, Kenneth Hill, Joan Higginson. Headmaster: Stanley Higham

Figure 29 National School photograph 1927

Bernard served in the war from the start in 1939. Joining the 3rd Ambulance Car Company Royal Army Service Corps based at Wolverhampton. During May 1940, he was involved in the evacuation of Dunkirk serving as part of an ambulance car crew. These crews were unarmed, their vehicles were marked with a large red cross their only protection against enemy fire.

It was on one such operation Bernard was taken prisoner and transported to one of the Stalag camps near Marienburg. His family had received a letter from him stating he was well but had to work hard. By October, he had died and was buried at a local burial ground, although notification of his death didn't reach his parents until two months later. After the war all casualties from the former POW camps were reinterred in the Commonwealth War Graves Cemetery at Malbork, Poland.

The Hinckley Times on the 13th December 1940 reported that official notification had been received by Mr and Mrs Sam Colkin, who were living in Forrester's Road, Burbage, that their son, Bernard had died whilst being held as a prisoner of war in Germany.

Figure 30 Home of Mr & Mrs Colkin, 10 Forresters Road

Burbage Soldier's Death in Germany

Official notification has been received this week by Mr. and Mrs. Sam Colkin, of Forresters Road, Burbage, that their only son, Driver Bernard Colkin, has died while a prisoner of war in Germany.

Pte. Colkin joined the R.A.S.C. as a militiaman and was serving in France at the time of the Dunkirk operations. He was then taken prisoner. Mr. and Mrs. Colkin had received a letter from him since he was taken prisoner, stating that he was all right but had to work very hard.

Pte. Colkin, according to the communication, died in October. He was very well known and highly repected in the district and much sympathy is felt for the bereaved parents.

Figure 31 Hinckley Times – 13th December 1940

Figure 32 Edward Colkin's grave, Malbork, Poland

Figure 33 Malbork War Cemetery, Poland

Figure 34 Edward Colkin's Prisoner of War Photo

PRIVATE DENNIS COMER

Service Number: 5891793
Enlisted: 5th Battalion Northamptonshire Regiment
Born: 1923
Died: Killed in action 29th November 1942, Aged 20
Memorials: Massicault War Cemetery, Tunisia Plot 4, Row A, Grave 11
Burbage War Memorial,
St Catherine's Church Memorial,
Hinckley War Memorial,
Regent Club Memorial,
Burbage Congregational Church Memorial

Dennis was born in 1923, the younger son of Sydney and Ada Comer. He was born and educated in Burbage; his family story is told on page 28. He married Mary Tamar Moore in 1941 and made their home at 140 Edward Street, Hinckley, they had two daughters the youngest being only 11 weeks old when Dennis died. Before enlisting in January 1942, he was employed at the Engineering Co. on the Watling Street.

The 5th Battalion was engaged in North Africa. On 8th November 1942, a combined Allied force made a series of landings in Algeria and Morocco. The Germans responded by sending a force to Northern Tunisia which checked the advance by early December. Dennis, caught up in this first wave of aggression, was killed on 22nd November.

Dennis is buried in Massicault War Cemetery in Tunisia, the cemetery contains 1,576 Commonwealth burials of the Second World War, 130 of them unidentified.

His brother Mick was also killed in fighting, in 1944, see page 29 for his biography.

After the war, Dennis' widow and children emigrated to Australia and the Comer family lost contact with them. In 2004, the families were put back in touch after a chance meeting on Remembrance Sunday. At the ceremony, Brian Simpson, a Burbage friend who had kept in touch with Dennis' widow met Iris, the younger sister of the two Comer brothers and was able to give her the contact details.

Right: Figure 35 Massicault War Cemetery, Tunisia

Burbage Man Killed in Action

PTE. DENNIS COMER

Hinckley people will sympathise with Mrs. Mary Comer, of 140, Edward Street, Hinckley, in the loss she has sustained by the death of her husband, Pte. Dennis Comer, of Burbage, who has been reported killed in action in North Africa.

Pte. Comer leaves two little children, one 15 months old and the other 11 weeks. It has only been a few months since he left this country, and the news of his death came as a great shock to his relatives and friends.

He joined the Army in January of this year, previously being employed at Engineering Co. on the Watling Street. He was 20 years of age.

His wife, before her marriage, Miss Mary Moore, was a former Hinckley carnival maid of honour.

Figure 36 *Hinckley Times 25th December 1942*

The Comer Family Story

Michael Sydney Comer (known as Sydney), the father of Dennis, was born in Wellsborough, near Stratford on Avon in 1885. In 1914, before going off to war, he married Burbage girl Ada Howkins.

The census records show that Sydney had a varied carreer including engine cleaner, coal miner and hosiery machinist. Soon after their marriage the couple started a family in 1915 with the birth of their eldest son Sydney Charles, with more siblings coming along after WW1, in the 1920s. In total the couple had two sons and five daughters, although sadly the youngest daughters died at only 2 and 6 years old. During this time they lived at 64 Hinckley Road, Burbage

By 1936, Sydney had lost two young daughters and his wife Ada, who died aged 34 years. Sydney and his family moved, before 1939, a little further down Hinckley Road, to 'Avon House'.

WW2 placed further toll on his life when his two sons went off to war. Having survived WW1, himself, he knew the cost of war and he must have dreaded the notifications he subsequently received that first his youngest son, Dennis had died, followed nearly two years later that his eldest, Sydney Charles was also killed in action.

Iris West (née Comer), never forgot her two elder brothers and visited both their graves in Italy and Tunisia before she died in 2008.

Figure 37 Dennis Comer Gravestone

PRIVATE SYDNEY CHARLES COMER

Service Number: 4862198
Enlisted: 16th May 1940 Leicestershire Regiment
Transferred to 1st/4th Battalion Hampshire Regiment 30th April 1943
Born: 15th August 1915
Died: Killed in action 15th September 1944, Aged 30
Memorials: Gradara War Cemetery, Italy Plot 2 Row E Grave 44
Burbage War Memorial
St Catherine's Church Memorial
Burbage Congregational Memorial
Liberal Club Memorial

Sydney Charles Comer, known as "Mick", was born on 15th August 1915, the eldest son of Sydney and Ada Comer. The Comer family story is given on page 28.

The family lived very near to the National School where Mick started in 1920. Growing up in the village he was a member of the Liberal Club and the Burbage Congregational Football Club. He married Cicely Daisy Allwood early in 1942.

PTE. MICK COMER KILLED IN ACTION

Pte. S. (Mick) Comer has been reported killed in action in Italy. His wife and eleven-months-old son live at 45, William Iliffe Street, Hinckley.

He is the eldest son of Mr. M. Comer and the late Mrs. Comer, of Avon House, Burbage, and his younger brother was killed in action nearly two years ago.

Pte. Comer had been in the Forces 4½ years, and went abroad 18 months ago. Before the war he was a well-known member of Burbage Congregational Football Club.

Figure 39 Hinckley Times 13th October 1944

Figure 38 Cicely Daisy Allwood

Mick enlisted in the Leicestershire Regiment on 16th May 1940 and was transferred to the Hampshire Regiment on 30th April 1943.

The manner of Private Mick Comer's death was conveyed to his wife in a letter written by the Company Commander, Major Dolman. Mick volunteered to carry important information back to HQ, but was killed in his gallant attempt, see pages 30 & 31.

Figure 40 Gradara War Cemetery, Pesaro, Italy

Mick was buried close to where he fell at Gradara Cemetery in the Province of Pesaro in Italy. The site was chosen as it contains the graves of casualties incurred during the advance from Ancona to Rimini, and in the heavy fighting around Rimini, which was taken by the Allies on 21st September 1944 a week after Mick had been killed.

HINCKLEY MAN'S GALLANTRY

Pte. Mick Comer

News of how Pte. Mick Comer, of Hinckley, lost his life in the fighting overseas has been conveyed to his wife, who lives at 45, William Iliffe Street, Hinckley, in a letter written to her by Major E. Dolman, the company commander.

In his letter, Major Dolman says: "Your husband was killed in action by ememy machine-gun fire in September. His platoon had been sent out to obtain some important information about the enemy. This information had to be sent back over the wireless set which was carried by and operated by your husband. The platoon got trapped by the enemy in an isolated house, and for some reason or other they could not get wireless communication back to me at company headquarters.

"Although the enmey had the house covered by machine-gun fire your husband volunteered to go back towards company H.Q. to try and re-establish communications and pass the information through. Unfortunately he lost his life in this most gallant attempt.

"The loss has been felt throughout the company, as he was popular with everyone. I always found him very willing and cheerful, and I miss him very much.

"His platoon commander tells me that when he was hit he fell at once and did not move, so he must have been killed outright and can have had no pain or suffering. When I saw him later his face was peaceful. He was decently buried that night by our chaplain. In due course I hope you will receive a photograph of his grave. I want you to know that he died gallantly, and like many thousands of others, doing his duty in the cause of freedom."

Figure 41 Hinckley Times 10th November 1944

Figure 42 Pte S C Comer Gravestone

The Fallen

From: Major E. DOLMAN, 1/4 Hampshire Regt.
C.M.F.

Dear Mrs Comer,

As your husband's Company Commander I write to you to-day to offer my deepest sympathies to you in your great loss.

Your husband was killed in action by enemy machine-gun fire on 14th September. His platoon had been sent out to obtain some important information about the enemy. This information had to be sent back over the wireless set which was carried by and operated by your husband. The platoon got trapped by the enemy in an isolated house, and for some reason or other they could not get wireless communication back to me at Company Headquarters. Although the enemy had the house covered by machine-gun fire your husband volunteered to go back towards Company H.Q. to try and re-establish communication and pass the information through. Unfortunately he lost his life in this most gallant attempt.

The loss has been felt throughout the Company, as he was popular with everyone. I always found him very willing and cheerful, and I miss him very much.

His platoon commander tells me that when he was killed he fell at once and did not move, so he must have been killed outright and can have had no pain or suffering. When I saw him later his face was peaceful. He was decently buried that night by our Chaplain. In due course I hope you will receive a photograph of his grave. I want you to know that he died gallantly, and like many thousands of others doing his duty in the cause of Freedom.

Once again, let me join with all ranks of my Company in sending you our sincerest sympathies in your irreparable loss.

Believe me,
Yours Sincerely,
E. Dolman.

Mrs S. C. Comer,
45, William Iliffe Street,
Hinckley,
Leicestershire,
England.

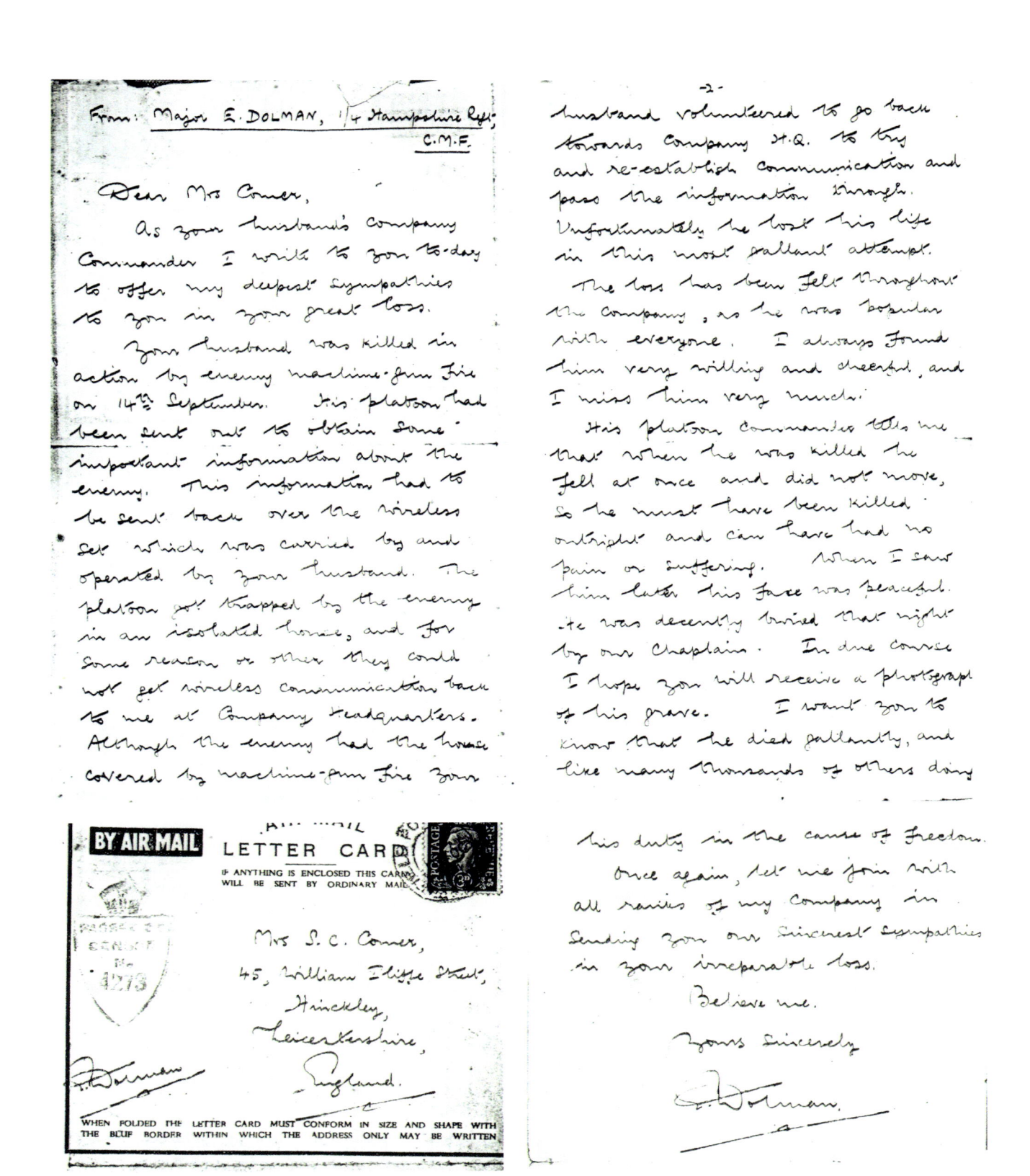

Figure 43 Letter from Major E Dolman informing of Mick's death

CAPTAIN EDWARD THOMAS CRUMP

Service Number: 66569
Enlisted: Royal Engineers
Born: 19th January 1904
Died: Killed in service 16th January 1941, Aged 36
Memorials: Dunton Bassett War Memorial
St Catherine's Church Memorial
Burbage War Memorial

Edward Thomas Crump, known as Tom to his friends, was born in Hinckley on 19th January 1904. His father, Edward was the Water Engineer & Surveyor for Hinckley Urban District Council, living at 23 Mount Road.

After his father's distinguished career in WW1, the family moved to Bristol where Edward Crump Snr was the Chief Engineer. Tom was educated in Bristol and followed his father's career as a surveyor working for the Ministry of Health.

By the mid-1930s, Tom's parents and sister Phyllis had returned to Burbage, residing at Tong Lodge in Church Street. By now, his father had established a private practice as a surveyor and architect. Tom subsequently became a surveyor with Leicestershire County Council.

Tom was popular in sporting circles. He played rugby for Hinckley and even when not playing, he never missed a match and would race up and down the lines urging his team on. As a cricketer, he was an enterprising batsman playing for Hinckley Town.

In 1939, he married Miss Elizabeth (Betty) Greenhough of Dunton Bassett where they made their home.

Figure 45 Tong Lodge, Church Street

Figure 44 23 Mount Road, Hinckley

Figure 46 Betty and Edward Crump

He had served in the Leicestershire Yeomanry for some years and on the outbreak of war was transferred to the territorial section of the Royal Engineers in which he obtained a commission. He was promoted to the rank of Captain, he trained in bomb disposal with The Bomb Disposal Group Battalion, Royal Engineers based in London. The average life expectancy in bomb disposal was estimated at ten to sixteen weeks. From 1939 - 1945, 55 officers and 339 men were killed, and 3 received the George Cross, for non-combatant gallantry.

At Christmas 1940, Tom visited his family and pregnant wife, Betty. On his return to London, he was killed by enemy action whilst fulfilling his bomb disposal duties on 16th January 1941.

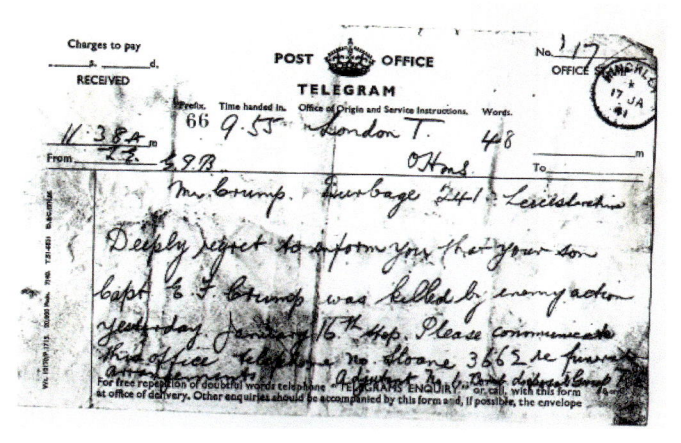

Figure 47 Telegram informing of death

On 26th January 1941 he was posthumously recommended for the award of the British Empire Medal, Military Division.

His body was brought back from London and rested in the Village Church overnight covered with a Union Flag. The funeral took place the next day and internment in Dunton Bassett Churchyard.

Figure 48 Dunton Bassett Graveyard

Figure 49 Dunton Bassett War Memorial

Tom's widow gave birth to a daughter Phoebe that summer. His wife eventually remarried and had a second family, but they never lost their ties with the Crump family and Phoebe remained close to her grandparents.

Phoebe died in 2005 and was laid to rest with the father she had never known.

SAPPER VICTOR CHARLES DAVIES

Service Number: 4856318
Enlisted: 275 Field Company Royal Engineers
Born: 6th April 1915, Birkenhead
Died: Killed in action 6th March 1943, Aged 28
Memorials: Sfax War Cemetery Tunisia, Plot VII, Row B, Grave 16
Burbage War Memorial
Burbage Liberal Club Memorial
St Catherine's Church Memorial
Holy Trinity Church Memorial, Hinckley

Victor was born whilst his father was serving in the First World War on 6th April 1915 at 2 Cardigan Road, New Brighton, Birkenhead. By 1919, his parents had separated and the young Victor and his sister, Iris, came to live with their maternal grandmother Florence Morant, at 7 Strutt Road and later at 24 Windsor Street, Burbage.

Figure 50 Victor as a baby with his parents and sister

On 11th July 1919, Victor and Iris were admitted into the Burbage Church School, the register states their former School was in Newport. The later registers show they left Burbage in 1926, but came back in 1927. After leaving school, Victor eventually trained to be a bus driver, firstly working for Robinson's Buses of Burbage.

In the mid-1930's, he met and married a Burbage girl, Kathleen Amelia Morris and set up home in Hinckley, to be near his work with the Birmingham and Midland Red Bus Company.

Figure 51 Victor and Kathleen

Victor had served in the Territorials from 1931-1935 and he knew, with his experience as a reservist, he would be called up early in the conflict. On 28th September 1939, two weeks after war was declared he enlisted with the Royal Engineers leaving his wife and two small sons, Peter and Michael, at 40 Strathmore Road, Hinckley.

On enlistment his army record, at the age of 24 years and 6 months states:
- Height 5 feet 9½ inches
- Weight 151 pounds
- 36½ inches chest
- Complexion fair
- Eyes Blue
- Hair Brown

On 10th December 1939, he was serving in France. The evacuation of Dunkirk started on 26th May 1940 and continued until 3rd June. Victor was one of the many successfully evacuated on the 31st May 1940.

Before leaving the country again, Victor had some home leave which ended on 9th January 1942. He bid farewell to his wife and two young sons for the last time. He arrived in Suez on 30th March 1942 to join the war in North Africa.

At the second battle of El Alamein, which resulted in victory for the Allied Forces on 3rd November 1942, the enemy were pushed into Tunisia. Most of the attacks with the Eighth Army took place at Medenine, the Mareth Line and Wadi Akarit in March and April 1943. On 6th March 1943, at the 176 Field Ambulance in Southern Tunisia, Victor died of his wounds.

Figure 52 Sfax War Cemetery Tunisia

Figure 53 Sfax War Cemetery, Tunisia

When the Burbage WW2 War Memorial was unveiled in 1948, the family were living at 31 Thirlmere Road, Hinckley. They decided, because his mother lived on Church Street. and Victor had spent some of his childhood living with her and had been married in Burbage, his name should be on the Burbage War Memorial. His name is also commemorated on the Holy Trinity Church Memorial, Hinckley.

Kathleen Davies received a War Widows Pension, which in 1943 was £1 15 shillings per week and an additional 16 shillings for the two boys, Peter and Michael. Victor's sons grew up in Hinckley, they are very proud of their father's sacrifice, and some years ago, Peter made the long journey to visit his father's grave at the Sfax War Cemetery in Tunisia.

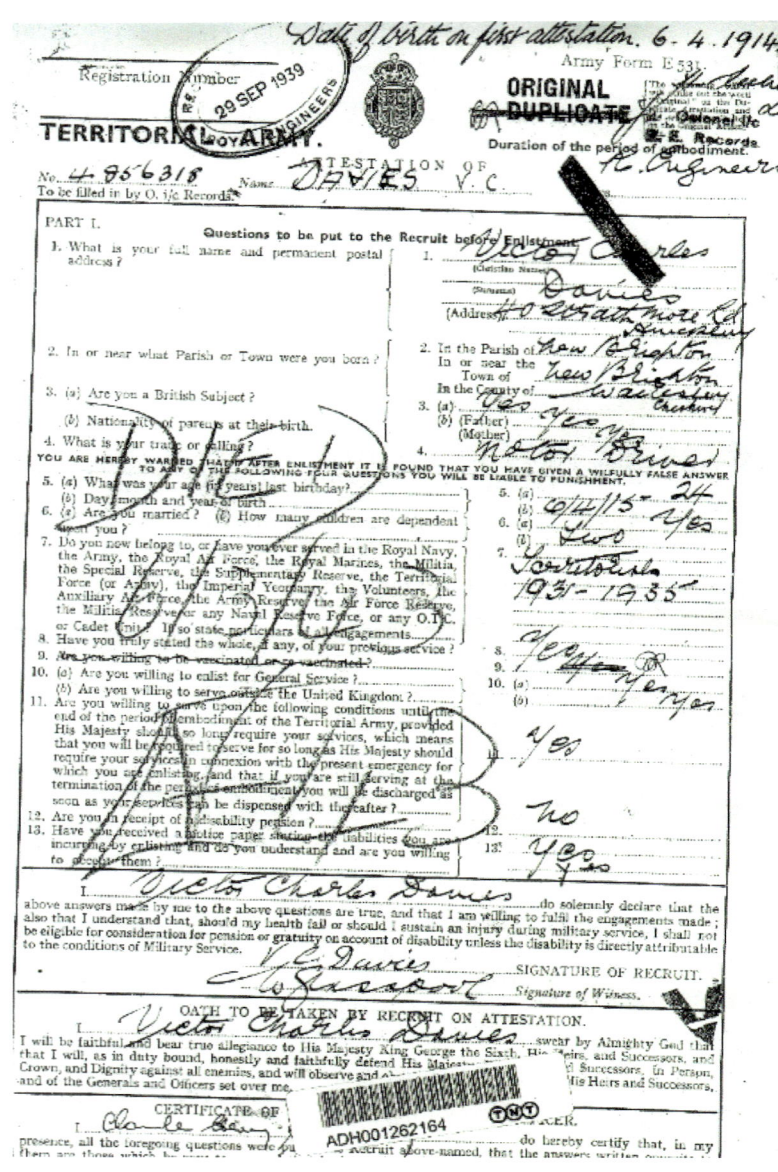

Figure 54 Army Attestation Form

DIED OF WOUNDS IN MIDDLE EAST

The Late Sapper Vic Davies

His many friends and acquaintances throughout the Burbage and Hinckley districts will regret to learn that Sapper Vic Davies, a former Burbage youth, whose wife and two small boys live at 7, Eskdale Road, Hinckley, has died of wounds sustained while serving with the Eighth Army in Tunisia.

He was 28 years of age, and had been in the Army since a fortnight after the outbreak of war. He successfully came through the evacuation of Dunkirk, and had been in the Middle East for about 15 months.

He was in the Leicestershire Territorials before being called to the Forces.

He was, in pre-war days, a 'bus conductor, being employed first by Robinsons, of Burbage, and afterwards by the Birmingham and Midland Red 'Bus Co.

His mother lives in Church Street, Burbage.

Figure 55 Hinckley Times, 2nd April 1943

Figure 56 Sfax War Cemetery, Tunisia

GUNNER HARRY DOBSON

Service Number: 956452
Enlisted: Bedfordshire Yeomanry, December 1939
Born: 17th June 1919
Died: 11th December 1943, Aged 24
Memorials: Burbage War Memorial,
Congregational Church Memorial,
Kanchanaburi War Cemetery Thailand – Plot 2, Row C, Grave 63

Harry Dobson was the son of John and Eleanor Dobson of 18 Flamville Road, Burbage. Harry was employed by Bennett Brothers Hosiery Manufacturers and Dyers of Southfield Road, Hinckley.

Figure 57 18 Flamville Road

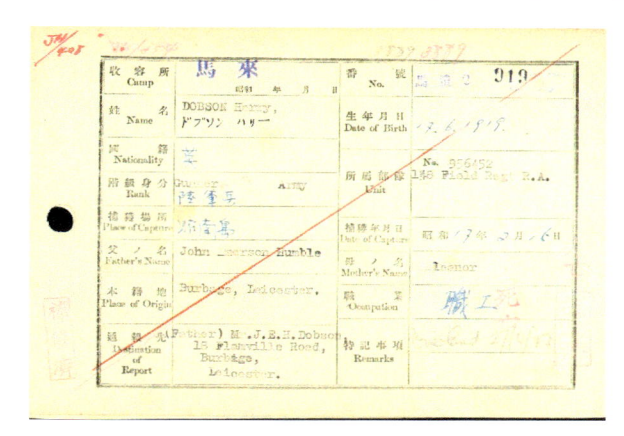

Figure 58 Prisoner of War Record

Harry Dobson, along with another Burbage casualty Jeffrey Tite, joined the 148th (The Bedfordshire Yeomanry) Field Regiment, Royal Artillery towards the end of 1939, after war broke out following the German invasion of Poland on 1st September 1939 and the declaration of war by Neville Chamberlain two days later.

Over three years, the two friends were transported worldwide and eventually became prisoners of war in Thailand, forced to build the notorious Thailand–Burma Railway. Their story, together with that of Harold Letts of Burbage, is told on page 100.

Harry was forced to work on the Railway until the time of his death on 11th December 1943, from chronic colitis. His father died at the Leicester Royal Infirmary on 22nd February 1944, aged 54, unaware of his son's death. Sadly, it took over 550 days for the news of Harry's death to reach his mother in Burbage, in June 1945.

Figure 59 Kanchanaburi War Cemetery, Thailand

DIED IN JAP HANDS

Gunner Harry Dobson

Mrs E. Dobson, of 18 Flamville Road, Burbage, has received the sad news that her only son, Gunner Harry Dobson, has died while a prisoner of war in Japanese hands. This information has just reached her. His death, from chronic colitis, took place on December 11th, 1943. Gunner Dobson, who was 24, was taken prisoner when Singapong fell. He joined the Forces with the militia in December 1939. Before the war he was employed at Bennett Bros., Southfield Road. His father has died since he was sent abroad.

Figure 61 Hinckley Times 20th June 1945

Figure 60 Kanchanaburi War Cemetery

ABLE SEAMAN HORACE HADLEY

Service Number: C/JX 410030
Born: 27th July 1911
Died: Lost overboard 6th May 1945, Aged 33
Memorials: Chatham Naval Memorial, Panel 80, Column 3
Burbage War Memorial
St Catherine's Church Memorial

Horace Hadley was born on 27th July 1911, the son of Thomas and Emma Hadley of Stockingford, Nuneaton. Horace married Florence Edith Buttell at Nuneaton in the first quarter of 1934. By 1939, Horace was employed as a General Labourer, (Aerodrome Heavy Work) and was living at 33 Balls Lane, (now Britannia Road), Burbage.

During World War II, Horace served as an Able Seaman in the Royal Navy and in 1945 was attached to the Motor Launch ML 445 from which he was lost overboard on 6th May 1945.

Allied Warships

HMS ML 445 (ML 445)

Motor Launch of the Fairmile B class

Navy	The Royal Navy
Type	Motor Launch
Class	Fairmile B
Pennant	ML 445
Built by	J.W. & A. Upham (Brixham, England, U.K.)
Ordered	29 Apr 1941
Laid down	
Launched	
Commissioned	12 Dec 1941
End service	
History	For disposal in October 1945

Figure 63 Details of ML 445

Horace is remembered on the Chatham Naval Memorial for commemoration of Royal Navy personnel with no known grave.

Figure 62 A Fairmile B Type Motor Launch

Figure 64 UK, British Army and Navy Birth, Marriage and Death Records, 1730-1960

Chatham Naval Memorial

The Memorial overlooks the town of Chatham and is approached by a steep path from the Town Hall Gardens at the end of King's Bastion. After the First World War, an appropriate way had to be found of commemorating those members of the Royal Navy who had no known grave, the majority of deaths having occurred at sea where no permanent memorial could be provided. An Admiralty committee recommended that the three manning ports in Great Britain - Chatham, Plymouth and Portsmouth - should each have an identical memorial of unmistakable naval form, an obelisk, which would serve as a leading mark for shipping. The memorials were designed by Sir Robert Lorimer, who had already carried out a considerable amount of work for the Commission, with sculpture by Henry Poole.

After the Second World War it was decided that the naval memorials should be extended to provide space for commemorating the naval dead without graves of that war, but since the three sites were dissimilar, a different architectural treatment was required for each. The architect for the Second World War extension at Chatham was Sir Edward Maufe (who also designed the Air Forces memorial at Runnymede) and the additional sculpture was by Charles Wheeler and William McMillan.

Chatham Naval Memorial commemorates 8,514 sailors of the First World War and 10,098 of the Second World War.

SARGEANT GEORGE HARRISON

Service Number: 4864964
Enlisted: 7th Battalion Leicestershire Regiment
Born: 17th February 1910
Died: 3rd June 1944, Aged 33
Memorials: Taukkyan War Cemetery, Myanmar, Burma
Plot 13, Row E, Grave 8
Burbage War Memorial
St Catherine's Church Memorial

George Harrison was born on 17th February 1910 in Cotes, Leicestershire, the second son of William George and Louisa Harrison.

By 1939, the family were living at The Croft, Bulkington Road, Wolvey, where his father was employed as a Roadman for Warwickshire County Council and George was a Hosiery Dull Finisher and a Special Constable for Warwickshire Constabulary.

Figure 65 The Croft, Bulkington Road, Wolvey

In the 2nd quarter of 1940 George married Eveline Joyce Chamberlain of 49 Lutterworth Road, Burbage and they made their home at Coventry Road, Burbage.

Almost immediately following his marriage George enlisted with the Leicester Regiment on 26th July 1940 and was assigned to the 7th Battalion.

In July 1940, the 7th Battalion was formed at Nottingham; its first role was beach defence. In September 1942 it set sail for India, where the Battalion was selected as the only non-regular Battalion for General Orde Wingate's Chindits Force. Wingate was known for his creation of the Chindit deep-penetration missions in Japanese-held territory during the Burma Campaign. In April 1944; the Battalion had been in Burma for 18 months, causing disruption with the Japanese communications and ambushing reinforcements.

On 31st December 1944, the 7th Battalion ceased to exist. Most suffered from exhaustion and disease such as dysentery and malaria. Many became hospitalised all over India. Those who were fit for service were transferred to the 2nd Battalion. During this period George developed a fever, he died on 3rd June 1944 and is buried at Taukkyan War Cemetery, Burma.

Figure 66 Chindit soldiers carrying a wounded comrade to be evacuated

Figure 67 George Harrison (Left) at his brother's wedding, (John James Harrison)

DIED OF FEVER IN BURMA

Four months ago, Mrs. E. Harrison, of Coventry Road, Burbage, received news that her husband, Sgt. George Harrison, of the Leicestershire Regt., had died on active service in Burma. Nothing further was heard concerning the circumstances until this week, when Mrs. Harrison received a letter from one of her husband's officers stating that Sgt. Harrison had died of fever and that he faced his death with the same cheerful gallantry with which a few days before he had faced the enemy.

Sgt. Harrison was the second son of Mr. and Mrs. W. Harrison, of Wolvey.

Figure 68 Hinckley Times – 20th October 1944:

Taukkyan War Cemetery is the largest of the three war cemeteries in Burma. It was begun in 1951 for the reception of graves from four battlefield cemeteries at Akyab, Mandalay, Meiktila and Sahmaw which were difficult to access and could not be maintained. The last was an original 'Chindit' cemetery containing many of those who died in the battle for Myitkyina. The graves have been grouped together at Taukkyan to preserve the individuality of these battlefield cemeteries. Burials were also transferred from civil and cantonment cemeteries, and from a number of isolated jungle and roadside sites.

The cemetery now contains 6,374 Commonwealth burials of the Second World War, 867 of them unidentified. In the 1950s, the graves of 52 Commonwealth servicemen of the First World War were transferred to Taukkyan, from outlying cemeteries where permanent maintenance was not possible.

Taukkyan War Cemetery also contains *The Rangoon Memorial*, which bears the names of almost 27,000 men of the Commonwealth land forces who died during the campaigns in Burma and who have no known grave.

The *Taukkyan Cremation Memorial* commemorates more than 1,000 Second World War casualties whose remains were cremated in accordance with their faith. The *Taukkyan Memorial* commemorates 46 servicemen of both wars who died and were buried elsewhere in Burma but whose graves could not be maintained.

Figure 69 Taukkyan War Cemetery, Myanmar

PRIVATE FRANK HOLYOAK

Service Number: 4862889
Enlisted: 2nd/5th Battalion Leicestershire Regiment
Born: 8th April 1913
Died: 22nd February 1943, Aged 29
Memorials: Enfidaville War Cemetery, Tunisia
Plot 2, Row C, Grave 13
Burbage War Memorial
Wesleyan Memorial
St Catherine's Church Memorial

Frank Holyoak was born on 8th April 1913, the youngest child of Joseph and Eliza Holyoak of 3 Lutterworth Road, Burbage. His father's family had run the Blacksmiths near the corner of Lutterworth Road and Lychgate Lane, Burbage. Four generations of Holyoaks had provided smithy services here, over a period of 100 years.

Frank's father died when he was 4 years old, and his elder brother Richard Harold soon took over the role of smithy in the family business.

Figure 70 (L to R) Richard Harold Holyoak, Mr Arthur Reeves and Mr Lissaman at the Blacksmiths

Although still living at the smithy with the family, Frank Holyoak took employment with Messrs. Chamberlain and Co, Hosiery Manufacturers of Burbage.

Frank served with the 2nd/5th Battalion of the Leicestershire Regiment during the war. The battalion became part of the Allied campaign in North Africa (see page 45). In March 1943, the family were informed that Frank was reported missing, whilst fighting in Tunisia. It was some months later that they received confirmation that he had been killed in action. He is buried at Enfidaville War Cemetery in Tunisia.

MISSING IN NORTH AFRICA

PTE. FRANK HOLYOAK
(Burbage)

Pte. Frank Holyoak.
Pte. Frank Holyoak, son of Mrs. and the late Mr. J. Holyoak, of Lutterworth Road, Burbage, is missing in North Africa.
He worked at Messrs. Chamberlain and Co., of Burbage, before joining the Forces, and was a keen cyclist.

Figure 71 Hinckley Times 2nd April 1943

North Africa Campaign

In May 1943, the war in North Africa came to an end in Tunisia with the defeat of the Axis powers by a combined Allied force. The campaign began on 8th November 1942, when Commonwealth and American troops made a series of landings in Algeria and Morocco. The Germans responded immediately by sending a force from Sicily to northern Tunisia, which checked the Allied advance east in early December. Meanwhile, in the south, the Axis forces defeated at El Alamein were withdrawing into Tunisia along the coast through Libya, pursued by the Allied Eighth Army. By mid-April 1943, the combined Axis force was hemmed into a small corner of north-eastern Tunisia and the Allies were grouped for their final offensive.

On 19th April 1943, the British Eighth Army, led by General Montgomery, launched its initial assault on Enfidaville. Determined to break through Axis defences, Allied troops faced fierce resistance. One of the most intense battles occurred on 20th/21st April, when Allied forces captured the vital hilltop village of Takrouna after brutal combat. Despite this success, the Axis defenders skilfully used minefields, artillery, and machine-gun nests to slow the Allied advance.

By 29th April, the Eighth Army was forced to pause its offensive due to the difficult terrain and strong enemy fortifications. However, the strategic importance of Enfidaville kept it in focus as the Allies planned their next moves.

The tide turned on May 6 with the launch of Operation Vulcan, a large-scale Allied offensive aimed at crushing the remaining Axis forces in Tunisia. This was followed by Operation Strike on 11th May, which delivered the final blow to Axis defensive lines. With their positions overwhelmed and supply lines severed, Axis troops in Enfidaville, along with other strongholds in Tunisia, surrendered on 13th May 1943.

The fall of Enfidaville marked the end of the North African Campaign, leading to the capture of over 275,000 Axis soldiers and paving the way for the Allied invasion of Sicily and the subsequent Italian Campaign. This was a pivotal battle, which resulted in significant casualties and at Enfidaville War Cemetery, 1,551 servicemen are buried.

Figure 72 Enfidaville War Cemetery, Tunisia

Figure 73 Wesleyan Memorial

Figure 74 Enfidaville War Cemetery, Tunisia

Burbage Man Killed in Africa

Pte. Frank Holyoak

Reported missing during operations in North Africa last February, Pte. Frank Holyoak, son of Mrs. and the late Mr. J. Holyoak, of Lutterworth Road, Burbage, is now reported as having been killed in action.

Pte. Holyoak worked at Messrs. Chamberlain and Co., hosiery manufacturers, of Burbage, before joining the forces and was a keen cyclist.

Much sympathy has been extended to his mother and members of his family, who had never given up hope that better news would be heard of him.

Figure 75 Hinckley Times 29th October 1943

SARGEANT PILOT FREDERICK JOHN HOWARTH

Service Number: 754182
Enlisted: Royal Airforce Volunteer Reserve
Born: 12th January 1920
Died: Killed in a flying accident 3rd September 1940, Aged 20
Memorials: St Catherine's Churchyard, Burbage Row 9 Grave 13
St Catherine's Church War Memorial.
St Catherine's Church, bronze plaque south side chancel wall.
Burbage War Memorial

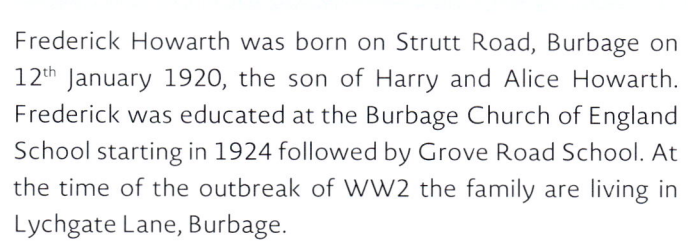

Frederick Howarth was born on Strutt Road, Burbage on 12th January 1920, the son of Harry and Alice Howarth. Frederick was educated at the Burbage Church of England School starting in 1924 followed by Grove Road School. At the time of the outbreak of WW2 the family are living in Lychgate Lane, Burbage.

At the age of fourteen, he moved on to the Hinckley Technical College and then Nuneaton Mining School where he studied electrical engineering. Having left college, he worked for Matkins Electricians then Messrs. Parsons and Sherwin and Co, the Ironmongers on Station Road, Hinckley.

In his spare time, Frederick was very active in the Scout Movement and spent a good deal of his time with the 4th Hinckley's St Marys Troop.

One of the most promising Rugby footballers in the district he played wing forward for Hinckley in the 1937-38 seasons.

In his late teens, he joined the RAFVR and was taught to fly Tiger Moths at Desford Airfield. When war was declared on 3rd September 1939, Fred immediately joined up and was sent to No. 1 Training Wing at Cambridge University in October 1939.

Figure 76 Former home of Harry and Alice Howarth, Lychgate Lane, Burbage

On the 18th December 1939, he was posted to No.7 Elementary Flying Training School at Desford. By May 1940, he was training to fly Harvards.

Figure 77 Harvard MK II

Having quickly made themselves familiar with one of the thirty-three Hawker Hurricanes at the station and local geography, new pilots were expected to adapt quickly to a series of tasks set by their instructors. These included what to do when vectored onto enemy aircraft and also how to deal with the situation of finding themselves under fire from the enemy. This involved arduous sorties flown as a pair, with the instructor and trainee fighter pilot taking it in turns to act as quarry and hunter.

During his second term of advanced flying, he moved to Royal Air Force Station, Sutton Bridge near Kings Lynn to train to fly and fight effectively in a modern fighter aircraft as part of a squadron. This included honing their skills on both offensive and defensive tactics.

A pilot's training course had originally been spread over forty hours, but this had been halved to twenty in order to prop up the losses that the squadrons had suffered over the summer of 1940. With the need for additional trainees continuing to rise, the pool of instructors did not keep pace. Consequently, those who mastered the basics of air fighting were sent out in pairs to practice amongst themselves. It was during just such a sortie that Frederick Howarth met with disaster.

On 3rd September 1940, a year to the day since Britain had entered the war, Frederick was flying Hurricane L1654 when he collided in the air with Hurricane L1833 piloted by Sgt. Karel Stibor (Czech) during an affiliation exercise between flights. Both pilots were killed and the aircraft completely wrecked.

Eyewitness accounts exist of the crash. Henry Allen, a land worker saw the two aircraft jockeying for a position of advantage over one another and much "stunting" was seen to take place to effect this end. One aircraft pulled up into a loop and during the final stages of this manoeuvre the collision occurred. The actual incident happened at around 600-700 feet and upon breaking apart both aircraft dived straight into the ground.

Alan Kew then aged ten, was tying up his shoelace before going to school when he heard the aircrafts' engines followed by the collision and subsequent impact with the ground.

He ran outside, but there was little to see except some smoke drifting away from the crash sites. Alan now owns the land where Stibor's plane fell. Fredrick Howarth's plane fell in the orchard of Bank Farm amongst the fruit bushes and plum trees.

Fortunately, both pilots' bodies were recovered. Sgt. Stibor was buried at Sutton Bridge Church near the airfield and Frederick Howarth was brought back to Burbage and laid to rest in St Catherine's Churchyard.

Figure 79 Plaque St Catherine's Church

```
TUESDAY, THE THIRD, SEPTEMBER
The schoolboy stooped to tie his shoe
His ear picked up the sound
Of stunting fighter aeroplanes
A mile above the ground.

Before his hand was on the latch
His breath caught in his throat
A bang, then screaming engines,
The final dying note.

Two more bangs as the aircraft hit
The boy was through the door
Just stupifying silence
No more the Merlin's roar.

The time was o-eight-twenty-eight,
September third the date,
The year was Nineteen Forty,
Two men had met their fate.

The boy to school went on his way,
One lace was still untied
Passed wreckage in the plum orchard
Where now a man had died.

The other 'plane fell over there,
Where still thin smoke did waft, Into
the cloudless azure vault
Above the broken craft.

Hurricanes, an old man said,
From Sutton Bridge for sure,
Just practising their deadly trade,
Eager to join the War.

He ran to school, no thought of play
A sadder, older boy,
His dreams to be a pilot,
Abandoned like a toy.

The lad has grown to farm the land,
Where once the wreckage lay,
And since has told us of the sight
That met his gaze that day.

The years have passed, the memories
fade, But always he'll remember,
The day he bent to tie his shoe,
Tuesday, the third, September.
```

Figure 80 Poem by Alan Kew

Figure 78 St Catherine's Churchyard

THE FALLEN

Hawker Hurricane I (L1833)
Flown by Sgt. Stibor on the fateful day

Figure 81 Hawker Hurricane I (L1833)

Figure 82 Grave of Sargeant Karel Stibor

Sergeant Pilot
Frederick John Howarth
R.A.F.V.R.

Aged 20 years.

Who was killed whilst piloting a Hawker Hurricane on patrol in the vicinity of St. Germain, West of King's Lynn, September 3rd, 1940.

Greater love hath no man than this that a man lay down his life for his friends.

Figure 83 Sargeant Pilot Frederick John Howarth

49

After the war, the family placed a bronze plaque (see page 48) next to one for John Lord, another casualty of WW2. Both were installed on the wall above the choir stalls where they had sat as choristers, on the south side of the chancel.

In September 1985, the members of The Fenland Aircraft Preservation Society undertook a project named The Saddlebow Hurricanes to recover the remains of the Howarth's and Stibor's aircraft. The wreckage of Howarth's aircraft was discovered some 11 feet down in the former orchard now a stubble field. The seat control column and head armour were recovered first then eventually the Rolls Royce Merlin engine.

After painstaking restoration, the Engine and some artefacts initially went on display at the Fenland Aviation Museum Wisbech. After the Fenland Aviation Museum closed in 2023 the exhibits were transferred to a new exhibition hall at the City of Norwich Aviation Museum.

Denis, Fredrick's younger brother became a pilot with 158 Squadron, survived the war, and lived for many years on Flamville Road, Burbage.

Figure 84 Denis Howarth

LANCE CORPORAL FREDERICK HAROLD HOWKINS

Service Number: 4861140
Enlisted: 1st Battalion Leicestershire Regiment
Born: 25th March 1917
Died: 23rd August 1944, Aged 27
Memorials: St. Desir War Cemetery, Calvados, France
Plot 5 Row D Grave 10
Burbage War Memorial
Wesleyan War Memorial
St Catherine's Church War Memorial
Bulkington Church War Memorial.

Frederick, known as Harold was the eldest child of Kate and Herbert Howkins. Born in Burbage and educated at the Wesleyan Day School, the family lived at Rye Nook, Lutterworth Road. Harold had three siblings, an elder sister Majorie and two younger, sister Elsie May and brother Ronald. Harold enlisted in the autumn of 1939 after leaving his job as a tailor's presser at Sketchley Dye Works.

Figure 85 Sketchley Dye Works

After basic training he was selected for further training in signals and communications skills which commenced in May 1940. Over the next four years he was posted to various places throughout the UK and rose to the rank of Lance Corporal.

Probably through their work he met Joan Marguerite Loveitt of Ryton, Bulkington. Joan was employed as a laundry ironer and lived with her widowed mother Elsie and younger brother Elson at 7 Wolvey Road, Ryton. Whilst on weekend leave from his then posting in October 1940 they were married at Ryton Methodist Church.

Joan continued working and living with her mother, Harold visiting his wife and family in Burbage when possible. Prior to embarkation for France, Harold visited his pregnant wife and they decided if the child was a girl to name her Ann.

Fortunately, Harold missed the initial D Day invasion of June 1944 and would have known of the success of this, however the battle for France continued until the end of August.

Figure 86 Wedding Frederick Howkins and Joan Marguerite Loveitt, October 1940

The Leicester Regiment records show that Harold's 1st Battalion Leicestershire Regiment landed in Normandy on the 3rd July 1944 and came under the command of the 147 Brigade of the 49th Division. The final stages of the campaign were hard fought, forging towards the Seine. In mid-August the advance toward St Desir a small village 4km north west of Lisieux in the Calvados region of Normandy began. The village population of some 1,500 was finally liberated on the 23rd August. Sadly, for the Leicestershire Regiment it was to be one of the highest death tolls of the Normandy campaign with the loss of 22 men including Harold Howkins.

Harold had obeyed his instructions that he had first written at the start of his training to be a signaller in 1940. 'The main job of a signaller is to obtain and maintain communications at all times and at all cost.'

His parents were the first to hear the news of his death and had to travel to Ryton to break the news to his wife.

Harold's daughter Ann was born some seven weeks later on 17th October 1944.

He is buried at St Desir War Cemetery, Calvados, France.

At the end of the war in 1945 a local group of people, who lived in the Lisieux region, adopted the new graves at St Desir Cemetery until the War Commission were able to take full control. The Collet family adopted Harold's grave and contacted his wife, Joan. This started a lifelong friendship with both families and their descendants, Joan first visited in 1947 and then took their daughter Ann at the age of six in 1950. This initial visit made a lasting impression on Ann, and she continued to make regular trips with her mother and Harold's sister, May. These visits ended after Joan's death in 1984.

BURBAGE L.-CPL. DIES IN FRANCE

The death has occurred, on active service in France, of L.-Cpl. Harold Howkins, elder son of Mr. and Mrs. H. Howkins, of Lutterworth Road, Burbage.

L.-Cpl. Howkins had been in the Forces 4½ years and went out to France shortly after D-Day.

His wife lives at Ryton, near Nuneaton, and his younger brother is serving with the Home Forces.

Before the war L.-Cpl. Howkins was employed at Sketchley Dye Works.

Figure 87 Hinckley Times 15th September 1944

Every Remembrance Day, Harold's siblings would place a vase of dahlias, Fred's favourite flowers, on the Burbage Memorial after the formal wreath laying ceremonies. This annual commemoration continued until sister May, his last surviving sibling, died in 2004.

The most recent memorial to the Normandy Campaign was constructed in 2021 to commemorate the 22,442 British who fell. This is the British Normandy Memorial at Ver-sur-Mer overlooking Gold Beach in Normandy.

Harold's name can be found on column 319 along with the 21 who fell at St Desir on the 23rd August.1944.

The Allied offensive in north-western Europe began with the Normandy landings of 6 June 1944. St Desir War Cemetery is the most easterly of the Normandy Cemeteries. For the most part, those buried here died in the final stages of the campaign, in pursuit of the German forces towards the Seine.

KILLED IN ACTION WHILE DOING A SPLENDID JOB

Corporal J. Hall, of the British Army of Liberation, referring to the death of Lance-Corporal Howkins, of Burbage, says he was killed in action while carrying out his duty—a job of signalling to keep open communications to enable the troops to speed on to their objective, which thanks to the splendid work of the signals, was taken according to schedule. "As a regular reader of the 'Hinckley Times and Guardian,' the contents of which I greatly enjoy," he adds that he desires L.-Cpl. Howkins to get his just recognition of dying as a soldier on the battlefield.

Figure 88 Hinckley Times 27th October 1944

The cemetery contains 598 Commonwealth burials of the Second World War. 78 of these graves were brought in from Chartres (St Cheron) Communal Cemetery after the war, together with the four First World War burials now at St Desir.

Figure 89 Joan & Ann Howkins 1951

The Fallen

Figure 90 St Desir War Cemetery, Calvados

Figure 92 St Desir War Cemetery, Calvados

Figure 91 1970's Visit to St Desir Cemetery

ABLE SEAMAN PERCY JARVIS

Service Number: P/JX 231329
Enlisted: HMS Excellent II, Royal Navy
Born: 19th February 1905
Died: 23rd November 1942, Aged 37
Memorials: Dely Ibrahim War Cemetery, Algeria
Plot 3, Row F, Grave 22
Burbage War Memorial
Hinckley War Memorial
St Catherine's Church Memorial

Percy was born on the 19th February 1905, the son of James and Mary Jarvis of Hinckley. At the time of the 1939 Census, Percy was employed as a Bus Driver for Midland Red Bus Co. and is living at 169 London Road, Hinckley with his wife Anne Elizabeth (née Merrick) and his three children Alan, Royston and Kenneth.

Percy enlisted with the Royal Navy and was assigned to HMS Excellent 11, a land-based gunnery school at Whale Island, Portsmouth. During his service he served in both the Mediterranean and the South Atlantic.

In March 1941, his ship was torpedoed and after drifting with a number of others for five days in an open lifeboat in the South Atlantic, he was rescued by a Spanish liner and interned in the Canary Islands.

After being repatriated, in the following September he sailed in a Malta convoy and was involved in the North African campaign, where Allied troops made a series of landings on the Algerian coast in early November 1942. From there, they swept east into Tunisia, where the North African campaign came to an end in May 1943 with the surrender of the Axis forces. Percy was killed during the initial advance on 23rd November 1942.

Percy is buried at Dely Ibrahim War Cemetery, Algeria. The cemetery contains 494 Commonwealth burials of the Second World War and 11 war graves of other nationalities. There are also 25 non-war graves, mostly of merchant seamen whose deaths were not due to war service.

Figure 93 Grave Text

Killed While On Convoy Duty

Able Seaman Percy Jarvis.

Able Seaman Percy Jarvis, of Hinckley, has been killed while on active service with the Royal Navy. A communication to this effect has been received by his wife.

It is understood that Jarvis, who has been serving in the Navy for the last two years, was on convoy duty.

Before joining the Navy, Jarvis was a 'bus driver in the employ of the Midland Red 'Bus Co.

He leaves three sons.

Figure 94 Hinckley Times 5th February 1943

THE FALLEN

1 NAME (Surname first)	2 PORT DIVISION and OFFICIAL NO.	3 BRANCH OF SERVICE.	4 RATING	5 SHIP OR UNIT.	6 DATE OF BIRTH.	7 PLACE OF BIRTH.	8 DATE OF DEATH.	9 CAUSE OF DEATH.	10 PLACE OF DEATH.	11 DECORATIONS (If any)
10. JARVIS, Percy	P/JX 231329	R.N.	A.B.	H.M.S. EXCELLENT II	19.2.1905.	Hinckley, Leics.	23.11.1942.	1	Algiers, Algeria.	

Figure 95 British Army and Navy, Birth, Marriages and Death Records, 1730-1960

A/B PERCY JARVIS WAS KILLED IN AIR RAID

It now transpires that Able Seaman Percy Jarvis, whose death was reported last week, lost his life in an air raid on war service. Official notification to this effect was received by his sister, Mrs. Dimmocks. Earlier news of his death was received by his friend, Olive Cawthorne, from his Lt.-Commander. Able Seaman Jarvis had arrived at his destination a short time previous to his death, and writing home said that he was very fit and well. His last letter was written on the day of his death.

A/B Jarvis was torpedoed in March, 1941, and after drifting with a number of others for five days in an open lifeboat in the South Atlantic was rescued by a Spanish liner and interned in the Canary Islands. After being repatriated in the following September he sailed in a Malta convoy last year.

Amongst the letters of sympathy received is one from their Majesties the King and Queen.

The two elder of Mr. Jarvis's three sons are at present living in Devon.

Figure 96 Dely Ibrahim War Cemetery, Algeria

Figure 97 Hinckley Times 12th February 1943

DRIVER LESLIE DAVID JONES

Service Number: T/10702368
Enlisted: H.Q. 1st Airbourne Division,
Royal Army Service Corps
Born: 1st quarter 1923
Died: 20th September 1944, Aged 21
Memorials: Arnhem, Oosterbeek War Cemetery, Netherlands
Plot 16, Row A, Grave 12
St Catherine's Church Memorial
Burbage War Memorial

Leslie David Jones was born in the first quarter of 1923, the son of Thomas William and Daisy Jones of 6¼ The Horsepool, Burbage. His father was a bricklayer and general labourer.

Figure 98 Cottages The Horsepool, adjacent the Congregational Church (now demolished)

Leslie attended the National School, Hinckley Road, Burbage along with his elder sister Vera Eileen.

Before joining the military Leslie was employed by Hunt & Co. a mineral water and drinks manufacturer of London Road, Hinckley.

On joining the military Leslie served with the Royal Army Service Corps as a Dispatch Rider, with the 1st Airborne Division.

Leslie was killed in action when a mortar bomb landed only a few feet away from him and was killed instantly on 20th September 1944, whilst the 1st Airborne Division were taking part in "Operation Market Garden" in Arnhem, Netherlands.

Figure 99 Hunt & Co bottle

Right: Figure 100 Hinckley Times 13th September 1944

DRIVER LESLIE JONES (BURBAGE) KILLED

Driver Leslie Jones

Driver Leslie Jones, only son of Mr. and Mrs. T. Jones, of The Horsepool, Burbage, has been killed in action while serving with the R.A.S.C. Airborne Division. He has been in the Army 2½ years and previously worked for Hunt and Co., mineral water manufacturers, of Hinckley. Much sympathy has been extended to his parents and to his fiancée, Miss N. Mawby.

A letter from his captain says: "He was killed outright by a mortar bomb, which landed only a few feet away from him. . . . He had been doing splendid work with great courage from the very start. . . . You may well feel proud of him. Those who managed to get back will never forget those good friends and comrades who were not so fortunate."

THE FALLEN

Normandy Landings

Following the Normandy landings of June 1944, the Allied advance through northern Europe was extraordinarily rapid and on 11th September 1944, the Second Army entered the Netherlands just south of Eindhoven, the first Allied troops to set foot in the country since its fall in May 1940.

Their next aim was to cross the Rhine before the Germans had time to reorganise after their recent setbacks, securing crossings over the rivers and canals that stood in their path at Grave, Nijmegen and Arnhem.

'Operation Market Garden' would involve the United States 82nd and 101st Airborne Divisions, the Commonwealth 1st Airborne Division and the Polish Parachute Brigade.

On 17th September 1944, the 1st Airborne Division began landing west of Arnhem, but German resistance, bad weather and problems with supplies and reinforcements led to heavy losses, and their objectives were not taken. They were forced to form a perimeter at Oosterbeek which they held stubbornly until 25 September, when it was decided to withdraw the remnants of the division across the lower Rhine. Arnhem Oosterbeek War Cemetery contains the graves of most of those killed during the September landings, and many of those killed in later fighting in the area.

There are now 1,684 Commonwealth servicemen of the Second World War buried or commemorated in the cemetery. 243 of the burials are unidentified and two casualties are commemorated by special memorials. There are also 79 Polish, three Dutch and four non-war (including three former Commission employees) graves in the cemetery. The cemetery was designed by P.D. Hepworth.

Figure 101 Driver Leslie David Jones Gravestone

Figure 102 Commemorating the Battle of Arnhem

Figure 103 Restored 1944 BSA M20 typical WWII Dispatch Riders Bicycle

Figure 104 Arnhem, Oosterbeek War Cemetery, Netherlands

Figure 105 Arnhem, Oosterbeek War Cemetery, Netherlands

57

PRIVATE RICHARD JOSEPH KEARNS

Service Number: 14556334
Enlisted: 2nd/5th Battalion, The Queen's Royal Regiment (West Surrey)
Born: 1924
Died: 26th February 1944, Aged 20
Memorials: Beach Head War Cemetery, Anzio
Plot XX, Row G, Grave 9
St Catherine's Church Memorial
Burbage War Memorial

Richard Joseph Kearns was born in 1924, the son of Richard and Mary Kearns of Lychgate Lane, Burbage. His father was a hosiery knitter and his eldest brother James a textile engineer.

Richard was a Private assigned to the 2nd/5th Battalion of The Queen's Royal Regiment (West Surrey) and died of his wounds on 26th February 1944 whilst fighting in Italy. He is buried at Beach Head War Cemetery, Anzio, Italy.

Figure 106 Regimental Roll

Invasion of Italy

On 3rd September 1943 the Allies invaded the Italian mainland, the invasion coinciding with an armistice made with the Italians who then re-entered the war on the Allied side. Progress through southern Italy was rapid despite stiff resistance, but by the end of October, the Allies were facing the German winter defensive position known as the Gustav Line, which stretched from the river Garigliano in the west to the Sangro in the east. Initial attempts to breach the western end of the line were unsuccessful. Operations in January 1944 landed troops behind the German lines at Anzio, but defences were well organised, and a breakthrough was not actually achieved until May.

The site of the cemetery originally lay close to a casualty clearing station. Burials were made direct from the battlefield after the landings at Anzio and later, after the Army had moved forward, many graves were brought in from the surrounding country. Beach Head War Cemetery contains 2,316 Commonwealth burials of the Second World War, 295 of them unidentified. There is also one First World War burial which was brought into the cemetery from Chieti Communal Cemetery near Rome. The cemetery was designed by Louis de Soissons.

Figure 107 Private Richard Joseph Kearns

The Fallen

Figure 108 Beach Head War Cemetery, Anzio

Private Richard Joseph Kearns

Figure 109 Pte Richard Joseph Kearns

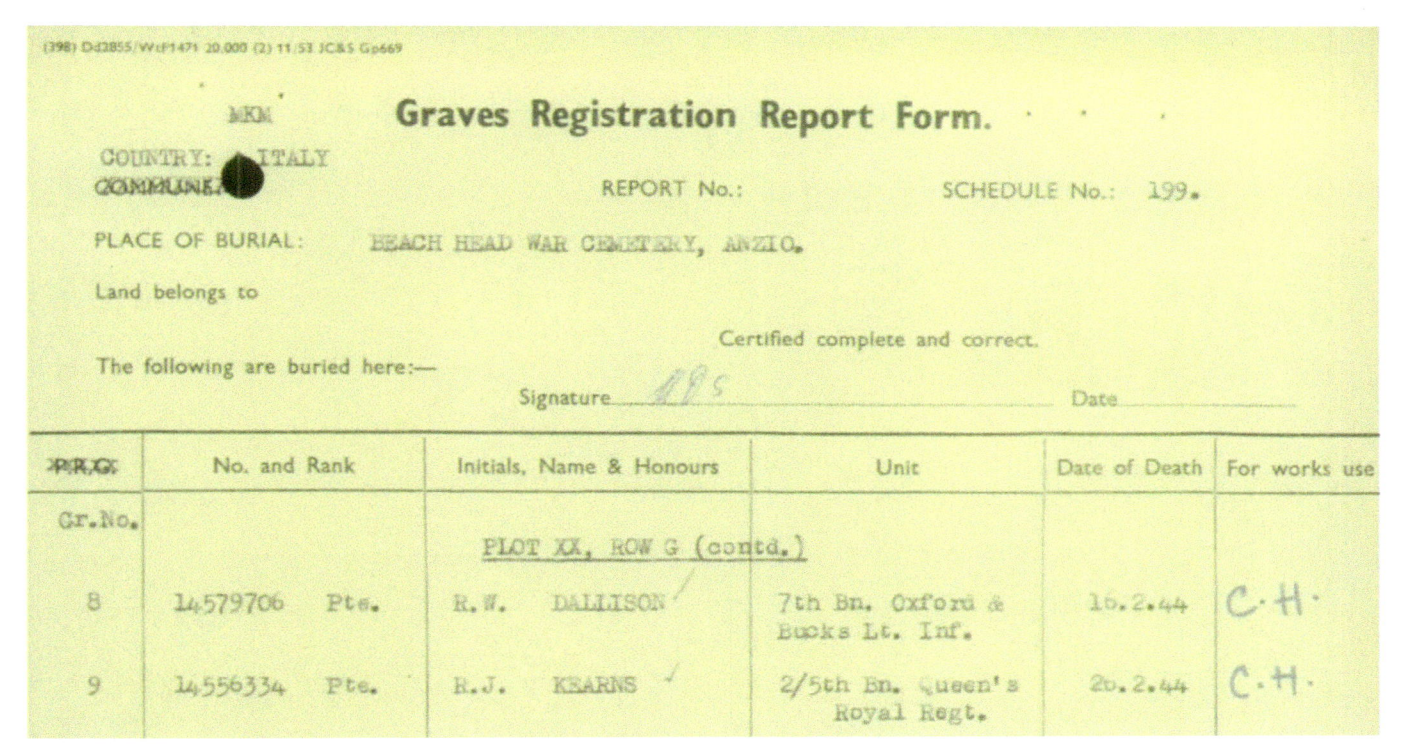

Figure 110 Grave Registration Form

SQUADRON LEADER SIDNEY EDWARD KELLAWAY

Service Number: 43448
Served: RAF Bramcote, adjutant to Polish Squadron
Born: 17th February 1901 Moseley, Birmingham
Died: 24th October 1946, Aged 45
Memorials: Burbage War Memorial
St Catherine's Church War Memorial

Sidney Edward Kellaway was born in Moseley, Birmingham on the 17th February 1901, the son of Percy Warburton and Harriet Mary Kellaway, he grew up at 91 Russell Road, Hall Green, Birmingham. Sidney was too young to serve in the early days of WW1 but was keen to serve, as soon as he was able.

Sidney enlisted with the, newly formed, Royal Air Force in the closing months of WW1. Private Kellaway 2nd class wireless operator (learner), started his military career on the 4th July 1918 at the Recruits' Training Wing, Blandford, Dorset. After the armistice in November 1918, he remustered as a general clerk. Promotion was rapid and after service based at Ruislip and Uxbridge he was promoted to Sergeant in 1922 and posted to Egypt.

Figure 112 RAF Depot, Aboukir, Egypt

Figure 111 Sphinx, Cairo, Egypt

His five-years' service in Egypt was at one of the most interesting times in modern archaeological history. Lord Carnarvon discovered the tomb of Tutankhamen in November 1922, Sidney visited the pyramids and the sphinx, which was then only half excavated.

By the early 1930s, Sidney was married with a young family. In 1937 with wife Barbara and children Eric and Margaret, he was posted to Aden serving as a warrant officer. Whilst in Aden (now Yemen) war broke out in September 1939, the Kellaway family made two attempts to get back to England. The women and children were quickly evacuated because of the fear of attack from Italian troops in Ethiopia, but when the danger subsided, they were sent back to Aden. Finally, in May 1940, after a treacherous journey the family made it back to England.

Figure 113 Photo taken RAF Aden

The RAF opened the new airfield, RAF Bramcote, in 1939. The base would become the home of three new Polish Squadrons together with the Operational Training Unit No18 (OTU18), Bomber Command. Group Captain Alexander Paul Davidson served as Officer Commanding (OC) at RAF Bramcote from June 1940 to November 1940. During his tenure, he was responsible for overseeing the formation of the new station's operations, including the establishment and training of the new Polish bomber squadrons.

When Sidney was appointed Adjutant for No. 300 Polish Squadron in May 1940, the family relocated to 1 Brockhurst Avenue, Burbage. In August 1940 he became the Adjutant for 305 Squadron.

On 19th February 1942, Sidney was made Administrative Squadron leader to OTU18. In February 1943, the unit relocated from Bramcote to RAF Finningley. Whilst in this post, he was mentioned-in-despatches three times: In June 1942, January 1943 and June 1943. The OTU18 was disbanded in November 1944, and by the end of the War in May 1945, Sidney had returned to Bramcote.

By 1946, Sidney's son, Eric, had joined the RAF and was stationed at RAF Cottisford. In Burbage, his wife Barbara become an active committee member of the Burbage Branch of the British Legion, Women's Section.

At this time Sidney's service in the Royal Air Force was drawing to a close and he applied to extend his service commission. On October 23rd 1946, after attending a medical board in London, which he successfully passed, he was driving home to Burbage when he was fatally injured in a road accident near Towcester on the A5.

The funeral took place at St Catherine's Church with full military honours. In the obituary in the Hinckley Times it states, "in all spheres of service he proved an efficient officer and was three times mentioned in despatches, the junior ranks had always found him a great friend, to whom they could always go when in trouble, never failing to find help and sympathy".

Sidney was so highly thought of that after his death the Commanding Officer of RAF Bramcote presented his widow with a silver salver.

This was engraved with all the names of the Polish Officers who were serving with the squadron at its formation in 1940, the names being arranged in the form of the Polish Flag. Commissioned in 1940, this was one of two such salvers, that were the prize possessions of the Officers' Mess at RAF Bramcote.

Figure 114 SQL LDR Sidney Edward Kellaway Medals

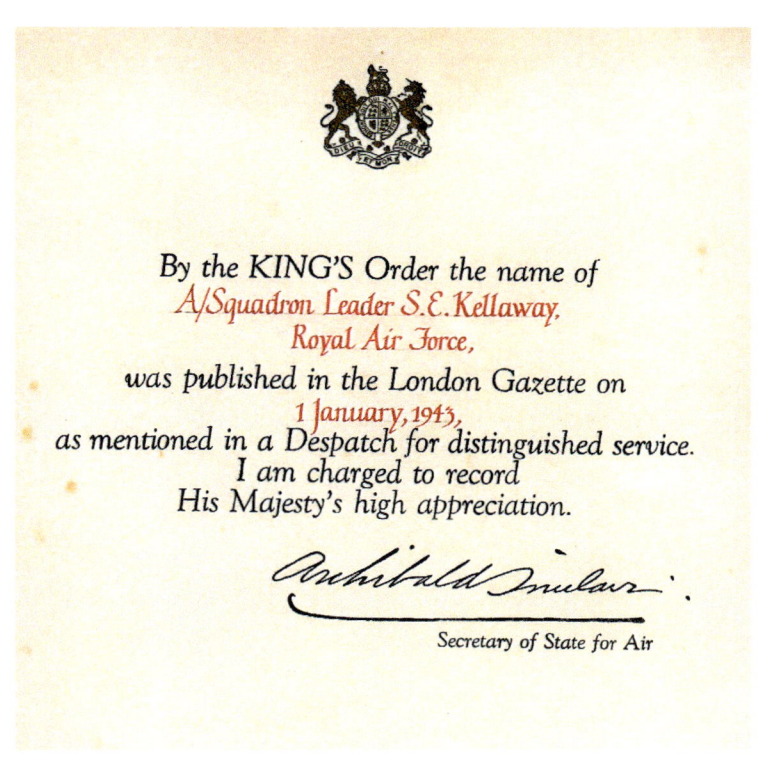

Figure 115 Mentioned in Despatch Certificate

GVI RI

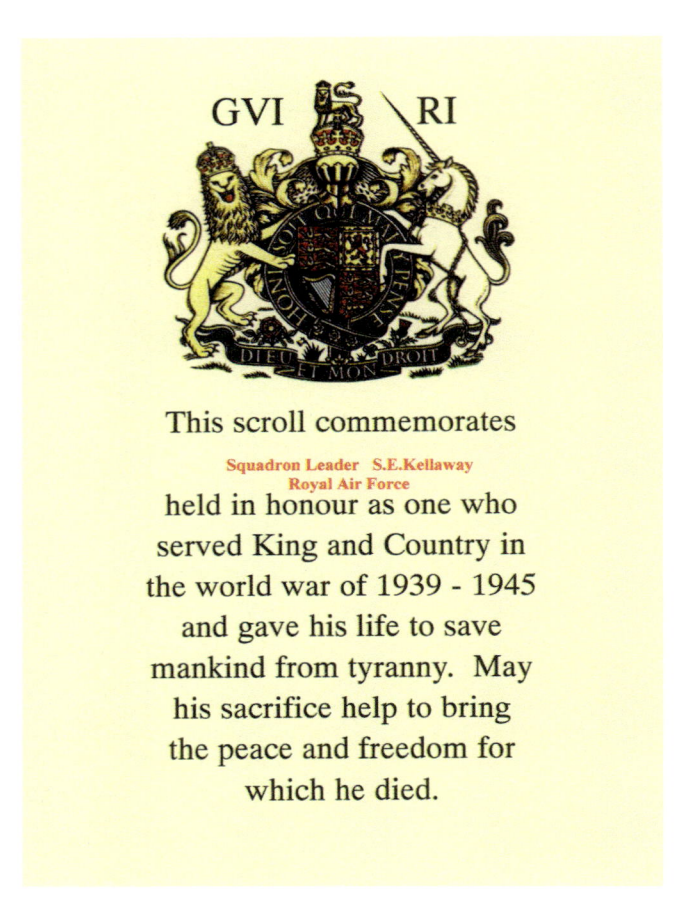

This scroll commemorates

Squadron Leader   S.E.Kellaway
Royal Air Force

held in honour as one who served King and Country in the world war of 1939 - 1945 and gave his life to save mankind from tyranny. May his sacrifice help to bring the peace and freedom for which he died.

Figure 116 Scroll of Honour

SQUADRON LEADER
S.E. KELLAWAY
ROYAL AIR FORCE
24TH OCTOBER 1946 AGE 45

WORTHY
OF EVERLASTING REMEMBRANCE
R.A.F. BRAMCOTE

Figure 117 St Catherine's Churchyard

LANCE CORPORAL HAROLD LETTS

Service Number: 4863375
Enlisted: 1st Battalion Leicestershire Regiment, attached to 3rd Corps Provost Company of Military Police (India)
Born: 18th September 1914
Died: 9th October 1943, Aged 29
Memorials: Kanchanaburi War Cemetery, Thailand, Plot 8, Row B, Grave 12
Burbage War Memorial

Harold Letts was the son of the late William Henry Letts, who was killed during the First World War whilst serving with the Grenadier Guards, and Annie Maria Letts of 11 Salem Road, Burbage.

Harold married Lorna Phoebe Farmer in July 1939 and they were lodging with Lorna's parents at 111 Clarendon Road, Hinckley. At this time Harold was employed as a Counterman by Bennett Brothers Hosiery Manufacturers and Dyers of Southfield Road, Hinckley.

At the outbreak of war Harold joined the Leicestershire Regiment and was attached to the Provost Company (Regimental Police) of 3rd Indian Corps.

Until the outbreak of war, the role of the 3rd Indian Corps was to defend the British Empire against internal threats against British rule and external threats from Afghanistan and tribal forces. During 1936 - 39 the British were involved in the Waziristan Campaign with the aid of Indian Forces defending territory against the region's fiercely independent tribesmen, most notably Mirza Ali Khan known as the Faqir of Ipi.

Before Harold's arrival, it is likely that the 3rd Indian Corps had recently shifted from defensive duties in India to supporting the British Battalion in what is now known as the Battle for Malaya—a campaign fought by Allied Forces against the Japanese Army. The British Battalion was formed by combining the 2nd Battalion, East Surrey Regiment, and the 1st Battalion, Leicester Regiment. It was commanded by Lieutenant-Colonel Charles Esmond Morrison of the Leicestershire Regiment.

The Japanese forces landed in the North East of Malaya on 8 December 1941 the day after the attack on Pearl Harbour. In 1941 Kota Bharu in North East Malaya was the base of operations for the Royal Air Force and the Royal Australian Air Force. The Japanese landed 5,200 troops, over 300 of the Japanese troops were killed and 500 wounded before the they finally took Kota Bharu town on 9 December.

The battle is notable for the Japanese use of bicycle infantry, which allowed troops to carry more equipment and swiftly move through thick jungle terrain. Royal Engineers, equipped with demolition charges, destroyed over a hundred bridges during the retreat, which did little to delay the Japanese. The retreat of Allied Forces through Malaya ultimately led to their presence in the defence of and ultimate capture at Singapore.

Harold became, as were two other Burbage pals Harry Dobson and Jeffery Tite, prisoners of war in Thailand being forced to build the Thailand – Burma Railway.

His story, together with that of Dobson and Tite, is told on page 100.

Harold was slaving, building the railway, until the time of his death on 9th October 1943. Harold's wife in Hinckley did not know the fate of her husband until November 1945, over 800 days after his death and more than 100 days after the war in the Far East has been declared over in August of that year.

L./CPL. H. LETTS DEAD

News has been received by his wife, Mrs. L. Letts, of 111, Clarendon Road, Hinckley, that her husband, L.Cpl. Harold Letts, died in a prisoner-of-war camp in Thailand, on Oct. 9th, 1943. The cause of his death was not stated. L/Cpl. Letts, who lived at Burbage before his marriage, and was a son of Mrs. and the late Mr. W. Letts of Coventry Road Burbage, was employed at Bennett Bros., Southfield Road, Hinckley, before joining the services. His father gave his life in the 1914-18 war.

L/Cpl. Letts

Figure 118 Hinckley Times Report 30th November 1945

Figure 119 Kanchanaburi War Cemetery, Thailand

Figure 120 Kanchanaburi War Cemetery

This old photograph was taken at the rear of the Weslyan Day School in Windsor Street, Burbage.
Back Row: Eunice Truslove, Phylis Paul, Connie Ghent, Evelyne Ghent, Edna Buswell, Rose Pither, Mabel Starkey, Mabel Mason, Miss Parsons (Teacher), Mabel Haddon, Elsie Chamberlain and Lily Fletcher.
2nd Row: Evelyne Green Phylis Wormleighton, Doris Starkey, Rene Reynolds, May Booth, Marjorie Howkins, Joyce Smith, Phylis Smith, Maud Cheney, Mabel Handley and Dorothy Chamberlain.
3rd Row: Arthur Johnson, Maurice Harvey, Frank Garner, Charlie Baum, Harold Letts, Fred Wright, Jack Farmer, Philip Pither, Gordon Wood and France Cook.
And Bottom Row: Joe Porter, Reg Yates, Dick Pay, Andrew Farmer, Ned Farmer, Ken Foxon, Reg Brandrick, Reg Wormleighton?, Les Moore and George Atkins.
The picture has been kindly lent to us by Mrs A. King of 40 Sketchley Road, Burbage.

Figure 121 Wesleyan Day School, Windsor Street, Burbage

Burbage All Blacks (left to right) (back) Herbert Moore, Harold Letts, Reg Buswell, France Cook, Albert Puffer and Eric Letts (front) Danny Merrick, Harold Cooke, Arthur Payne, Arthur Green and Tommy Woodward.

Figure 122 Burbage All Blacks

AIRCRAFTSMAN KENNETH BERT LOCKTON

Enlisted: Royal Air Force
Born: 1st Quarter 1922
Died: 8th April 1945, Aged 23
Memorials: Burbage War Memorial
St Catherine's Church Memorial
Holy Trinity Memorial, Hinckley
Regents Club Memorial (now held by the At Risks Memorials Project)

Kenneth Bert Lockton was born in the first quarter of 1922, the youngest son of Bert and Elise May Lockton of 16 Sketchley Hill Cottages, Burbage. His father was a Hosiery Dyer and his mother a Retail Shopkeeper. Kenneth attended the Hinckley Grammar School from 1933 to 1938.

In late 1942, he joined the Royal Air Force as an Aircraftsman. On the 23rd October 1943, Kenneth married Joan Mary Cash, at the Holy Trinity Church, Hinckley. Joan was born in Lincolnshire, although her parents had since moved to Hinckley.

Kenneth was invalided out of the RAF in November 1944, due to illness. The Hinckley Grammar School Magazine reported that, "Unfortunately, he did not make a full recovery and after a long illness he passed away in March 1945. He was quiet and of reliable disposition; he never complained and bore his illness bravely. Our sympathy is extended to his parents and family."

He died of cancer on 8th April 1945 and is buried at Hinckley Cemetery, Ashby Road, Hinckley.

Figure 123 Hinckley Cemetery, Ashby Road, Hinckley

Figure 124 Regent Club Memorial (held by At Risk War Memorials Project)

Figure 125 Gravestone Ashby Road Cemetery

WARRANT OFFICER JOHN LORD

Service Number: 955266
Enlisted: 405th (RCAF) Squadron Royal Air Force Volunteer Reserve
Born: 6th December 1918
Died: 22nd April 1945, Aged 26
Memorials: Berlin 1939-1945 War Cemetery, Brandenburg, Germany - Plot 2, Row N, Grave 7
Burbage War Memorial
St Catherine's Church Memorial
Individual Plaque St Catherine's South Side Chancel

John Lord was born on 6th December 1918 at Diamond Cottage, Coventry Road, Burbage, the eldest child of Ernest and Ada Lord (née Baum). Ernest was a hosiery hand. John grew up in the village starting at the Burbage National School in January 1924. John was well known in the Hinckley area being a regular player for Hinckley United Rugby Club.

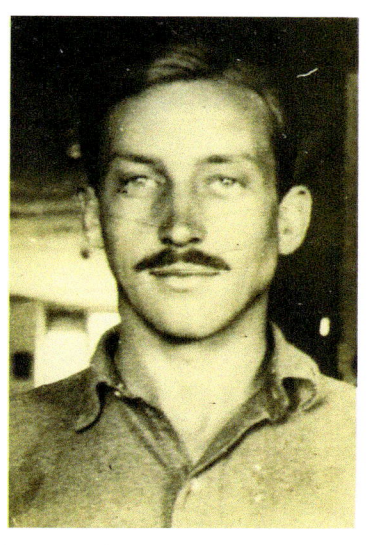

Figure 127 POW Photograph received by family

Figure 126 National School Photograph

On the outbreak of war in 1939, John joined the RAF and was posted to a base in Scotland. As an observer, he flew missions on bombing raids over Germany. On one such mission in 1941 his plane came down, he was captured and taken prisoner of war.

Although a prisoner, the family hoped he would be relatively safe. Letters were exchanged and parcels sent via the Red Cross. The family even had a photograph sent from a POW camp that shows him looking well.

PAGE FOUR

LOCAL SERVICE CASUALTIES

MARCHING PRISONERS ATTACKED IN ERROR: BURBAGE MAN DIES

THE end of the war in Europe brought sad news for a Burbage family. Mr. and Mrs. Ernest Lord, of High View, Coventry-road, Burbage, had learned of the relief of the prison camp in which their only son, Warrant Officer Observer John Lord, had been interned, and were awaiting news of his homecoming. Instead, they learned that he had died of wounds during a long march from one camp to another.

While on the march, the prisoners were mistaken for enemy troops and were attacked by Allied bombers. Lord and a number of his comrades receiving wounds.

Lord was well-known in the Hinckley locality, being a regular playing member of Hinckley RFC. Before joining the RAF he was employed at Sketchley Dye Works. He was taken prisoner during a bombing operation in 1941.

Figure 128 Leicester Evening Mail 11th May 1945

In April 1945, the family learned of the relief of the prison camp at which he had been interned and were awaiting news of his homecoming. Instead, they learned that he had died of wounds during a long march from one camp to another. While on the march, the prisoners were mistaken for enemy troops and were attacked by Allied bombers, John and a number of his comrades receiving wounds. Some of the prisoners had been forced marched from camps in Poland to Germany in front of the advancing Russians.

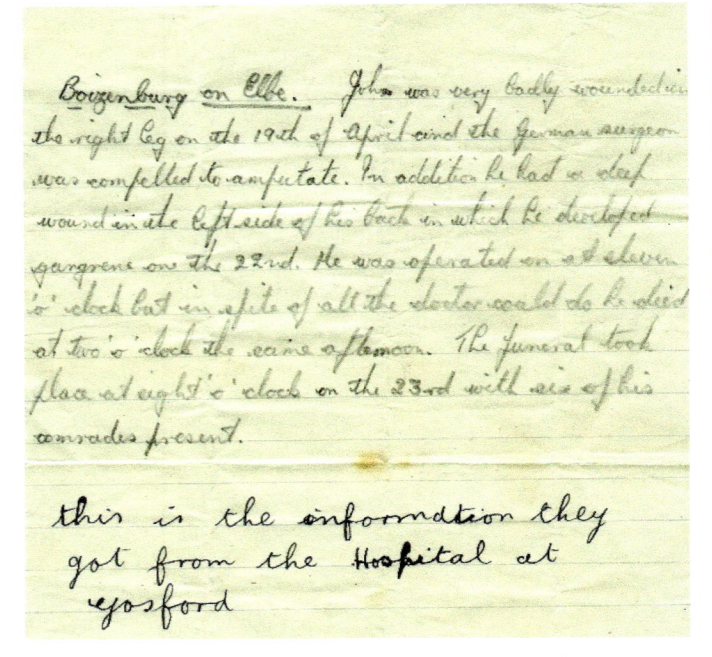

Figure 129 Letter received by the family about John Lord's Death

Figure 131 1939 – 1945 War Cemetery, Berlin

John was taken to Boizenburg on Elbe. He was badly wounded in the right leg on the 19th April and the German surgeon was compelled to amputate. In addition, he had a deep wound on the left side of his back, which became gangrenous on the 22nd April. He was operated on at 11 am, that day. Although the doctors did all they could for him, he died at 2 pm the same afternoon. His funeral took place the following day at 8 am with six of his comrades in attendance.

Figure 130 Army Graves Service notification of cross

Figure 132 Temporary Grave Cross

The Fallen

Figure 133 Warrant Officer John Lord Gravestone

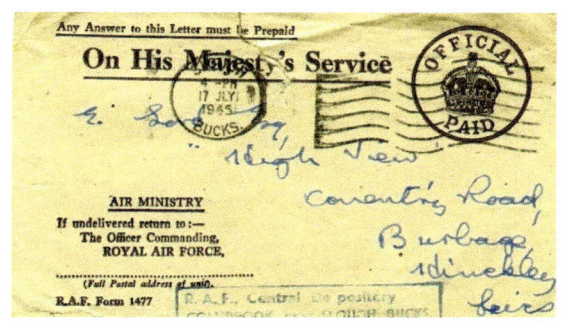

Figure 134 Air Ministry notification envelope

Figure 135 St Catherine's Church

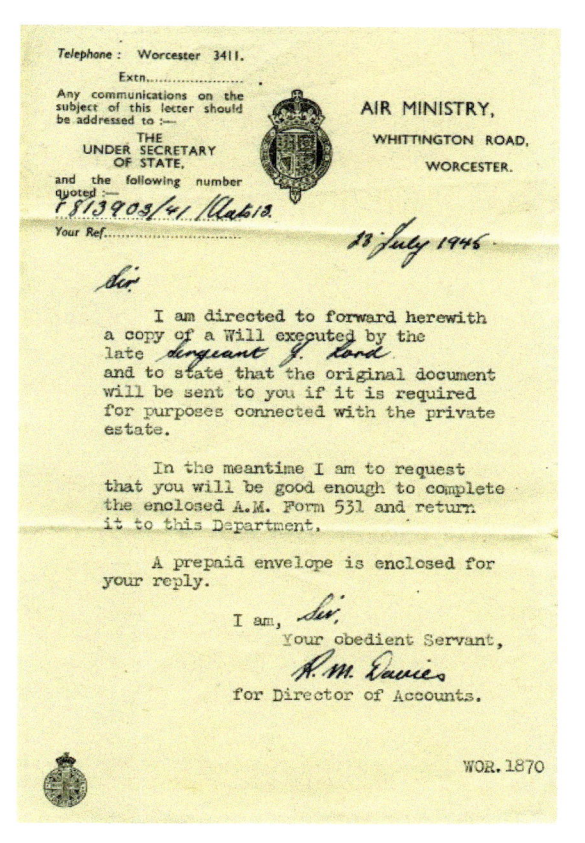

Figure 136 Air Ministry notification of Will

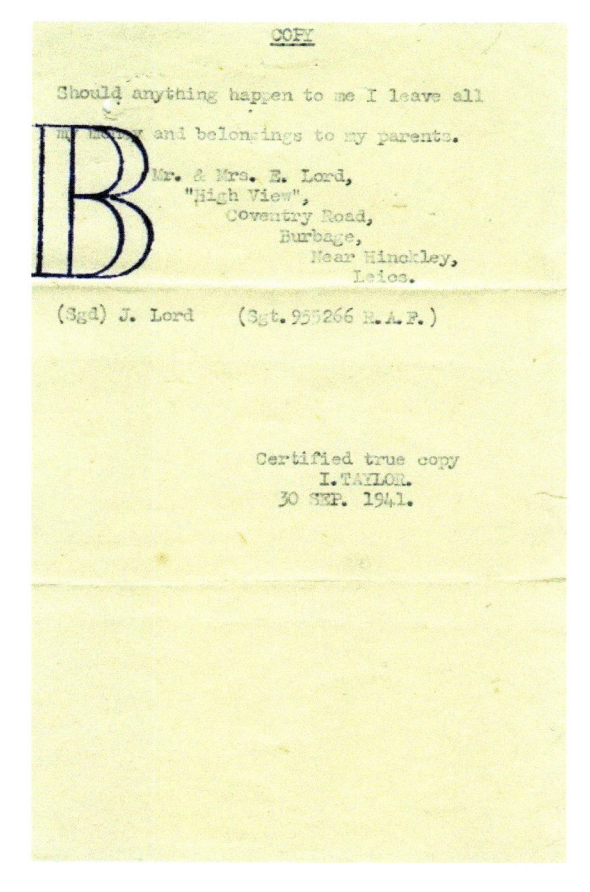

Figure 137 John Lord's Will

Figure 138 John Lord with his squadron in Scotland

Figure 139 Warrant Officer John Lord

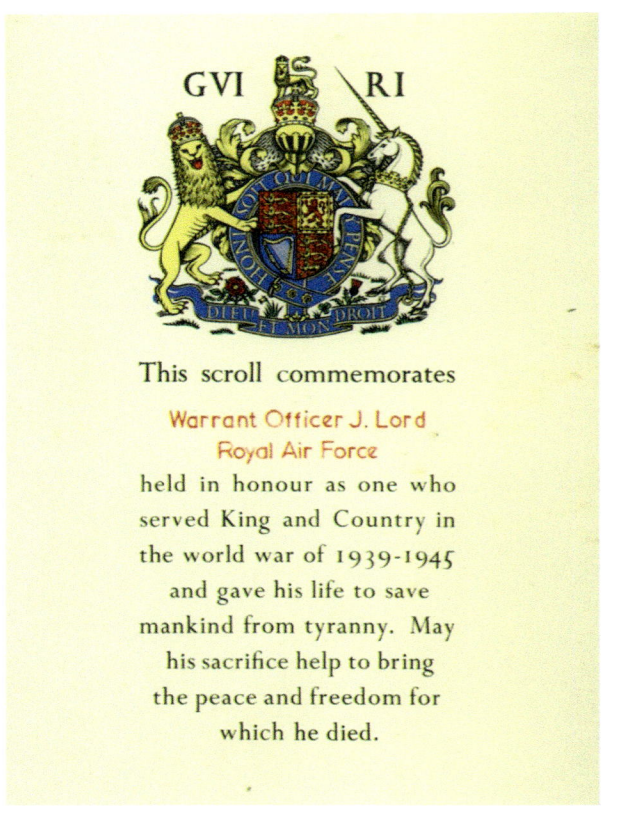

Figure 140 Scroll of Honour

This scroll commemorates

Warrant Officer J. Lord
Royal Air Force

held in honour as one who served King and Country in the world war of 1939-1945 and gave his life to save mankind from tyranny. May his sacrifice help to bring the peace and freedom for which he died.

AIRCRAFTSMAN 1ST CLASS STANLEY RICHARD LOUNT

Service Number: 1164291
Enlisted: Royal Air Force Volunteer Reserve
Born: 22nd June 1921
Died: 17th February 1941, Aged 19
Memorials: St Peter's Church, Aston Flamville- Row 1 Grave 1
Burbage War Memorial
Hinckley Grammar School Memorial

Stanley Richard Lount was born on 22nd June 1921, the son of Thomas William and Ethel Winnifred Lount of Aston Flamville, where his father was employed as a farm labourer. Stanley attended the National School in Burbage along with his older siblings Herbert William, Ethel May, Thomas Henry and Muriel Amy.

On leaving the National School, Stanley attended the Hinckley Grammar School from 1932 to 1937, and prior to joining the RAF was employed in the laboratory of Messrs. John Ellis and Sons of Stoney Stanton.

Stanley death is registered at Sleaford, where he was most likely to have been serving nearby at RAF Cranwell, he died on 17th February 1941 as a result of an illness.

He is laid to rest near his family home at St Peter's Church, Aston Flamville.

Figure 141 Gravestone, St Peter's Church, Aston Flamville

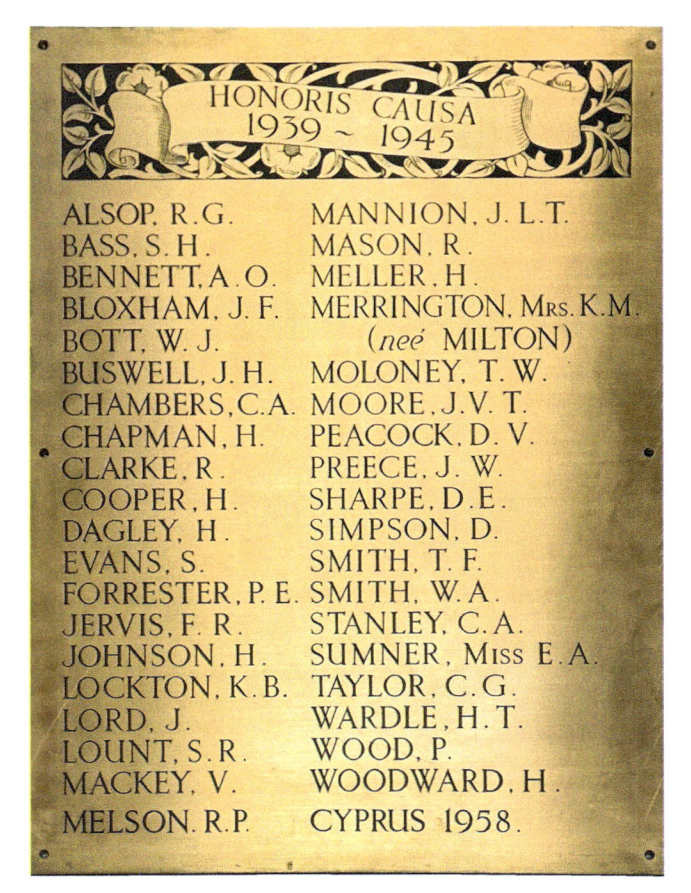

Figure 142 Hinckley Grammar School Memorial

Above: Figure 143 Graves Registration Report

Stanley's death, at the age of only 19 years, was reported in the Hinckley Times on the 21st February 1941. His funeral was held at St Peter's Church, Aston Flamville on Friday 21st February 1941 when his body was interred in the churchyard.

> **Hinckley Grammar School Magazine**
>
> *In the summer of 1941, the Hinckley Grammar School Magazine published an obituary for Stanley repeated below:*
>
> "Stanley Lount died on February 17th 1941 as a result of an illness contracted whilst serving in the RAF. He had been in the RAF for nearly a year and had been most successful in his examinations and was popular with his fellow men. Before joining the RAF, he was employed in the Laboratory of Messrs. John Ellis and Sons, Stoney Stanton, where he distinguished himself by his sound and conscientious work. At school he took advantage of all that was offered, playing a good game of Rugby football, where he was noted for tackling and a sound game of cricket and he also helped to make the 1937 Camp at Salcombe a success."

Burbage Airman's Death

THE LATE A/C S. R. LOUNT

It is with regret that we record the death, which occurred at an R.A.F. hospital on Monday, of A/C Stanley Richard Lount, younger son of Mrs. and the late Mr. T. Lount, of Aston Lane, Burbage.

Deceased, who was 19 years of age, was an old Hinckleyan, and had been in the R.A.F. for the past nine months.

He was a keen sportsman and was well known in the Hinckley district for his sporting activities. He played cricket for the Hinckley Amateurs and also took part with great distinction in the games while at the Grammar School.

He was formerly employed at Messrs. John Ellis Ltd., of Stoney Stanton.

The funeral takes place in the Aston Flamville Churchyard this afternoon (Friday).

Left: Figure 144 Hinckley Times - 21st February 1941

PRIVATE FRANK MOORE

Service Number: 555588
Enlisted: Sherwood Foresters transferred to Royal Army Ordnance Corp
Born: July 1913
Died: 10th July 1945, Aged 32
Memorials: St Catherine's Churchyard, Burbage Row 2 Grave 3
St Catherine's Church Memorial
Burbage War Memorial

Frank Moore was the third of the five children of George Harold Murray and Lucy Moore. At the time of the 1911 census, the family were living at 83 Princess Road, Leicester and by the 1939 census they were resident at Swallow Cottage, Lutterworth Road, Burbage. His father was a Director of Moore, Eady & Murcott Goode Limited, Hosiery Manufacturers with factories in Leicester, Derby, Hinckley, Burbage and Countesthorpe.

Figure 145 Swallow Cottage, Lutterworth Road, Burbage

Frank was educated at Brighton College Independent School, Brighton.

Frank joined the Sherwood Foresters in 1936 and during his service was transferred to the Royal Army Ordnance Corps. He was present at Dunkirk in France during May 1940 and during the Siege of Tobruk in Libya during 1942 where he was taken prisoner by the Germans. He was transferred to Campo Concentramento 53 at Sforzacosta, Macerata in Italy and then on to Stalag 344 at Lambinowice, Opolskie, Poland.

He was liberated by the Allies in April 1945 and repatriated to the UK. He died on 10th July 1945 at Queen Elizabeth Hospital, Birmingham from an illness contracted whilst held prisoner in Poland.

DEATH OF MR. FRANK MOORE

SON OF MRS. AND THE LATE MR. HAROLD MOORE, OF BURBAGE

Taken prisoner at Tobruk in 1942, and in enemy hands until his liberation at the end of April, Pte. Frank Moore, second son of the late Mr. Harold Moore and Mrs. Moore, of Swallow Cottage, Burbage, died on Tuesday in Queen Elizabeth Hospital, Birmingham, from an illness contracted while in a prison camp.

Pte. Moore, whose father was managing director of Messrs. Moore Eady and Murcott Goode, of Leicester and Hinckley, and whose grandfather, the late Mr. Frank Moore, was one of the leading industrialists of the Midlands, and chairman of the Leicester Chamber of Commerce, joined the army in 1936, and saw extensive service in the Middle East.

He was 32, and in his pre-army days played rugger for Hinckley Rugby F.C., and cricket for Burbage. He was extremely well known and popular in the Hinckley district.

The funeral is taking place in the Burbage Churchyard tomorrow morning.

Figure 146 Hinckley Times 13th July 1945

Figure 147 Frank Moore

Figure 149 St Catherine's Churchyard, Burbage

Figure 148 Frank Moore

MOORE Frank of Swallow Cottage Burbage **Leicestershire** died 10 July 1945 at The Queen Elizabeth Hospital Birmingham Administration (with Will) **London** 26 July to Lucy Moore widow. Effects £666 0s. 5d.

Figure 150 Probate Record

FLIGHT LIEUTENANT GEORGE WILLIAM NICKERSON MM

Service Number: 100738
Enlisted: Royal Air Force
Born: 10th March 1899
Died: 31st July 1943, Aged 44
Memorials: Montgomery Oakwood Cemetery Annex, Alabama, USA – Plot N, Lot 94, Grave 3
Burbage War Memorial
St Catherine's Church Memorial
Burbage Liberal Club Memorial

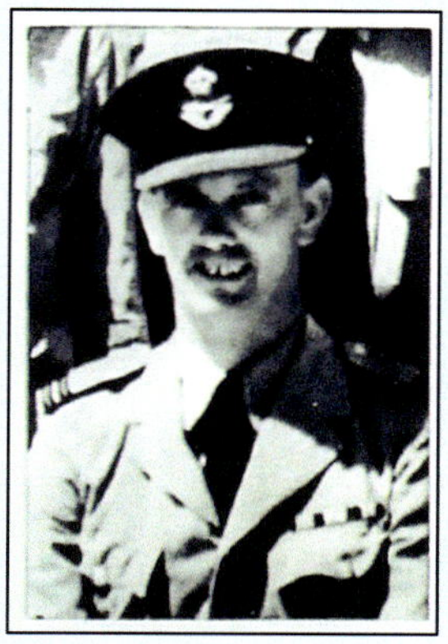

George William Nickerson was born on 10th March 1899, the second son of William and Mary Nickerson. The birth was registered in Nottingham and by the time of the 1901 Census they were living at 24 Charles Street, Little Gonerby, Grantham where his father was employed as a tailor. By the time of the 1911 Census the family had relocated to 57 Elmville Avenue, Scarborough where his father, William, continued his trade as a tailor.

George would have been eligible for conscription at the age of eighteen, in March 1917. A Medal Card exists for Private George William Nickerson in the Lincolnshire Regiment for the Victory and British Medals from World War One, but not the 1914 – 15 Star for which George would have been too young.

During his World War One service George was also awarded the Military Medal. George was promoted to Sergeant and became Unit Accountant from July 1919 until he left the Army in June 1920.

On 30th July 1921 George married Florence Mary Morris at Grantham and they went to live with his wife's parents at 19 Oxford Street, Grantham. They had a son Clifford Noel W Nickerson on 5th July 1924 and the birth was registered in Grimsby.

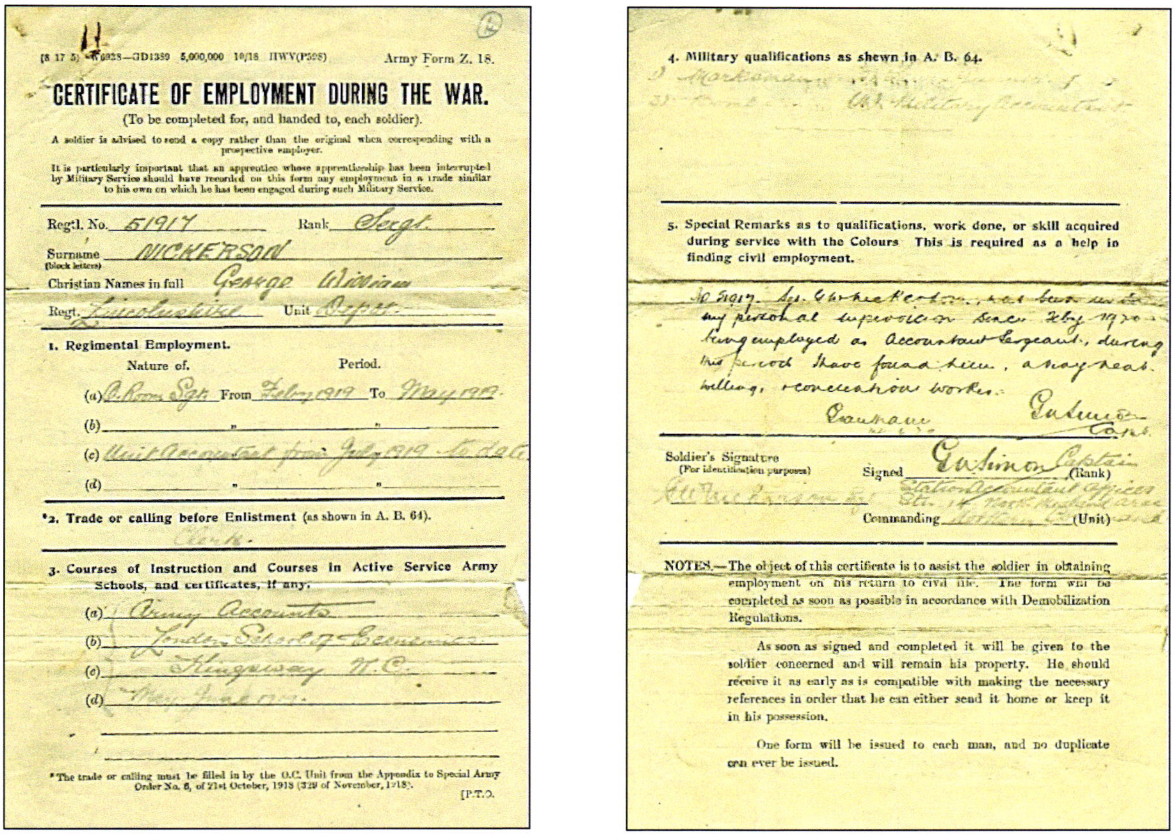

(8 17 5) W6928—GD1389 5,000,000 10/18 HWV(P598) Army Form Z. 18.

CERTIFICATE OF EMPLOYMENT DURING THE WAR.

(To be completed for, and handed to, each soldier).

A soldier is advised to send a copy rather than the original when corresponding with a prospective employer.

It is particularly important that an apprentice whose apprenticeship has been interrupted by Military Service should have recorded on this form any employment in a trade similar to his own on which he has been engaged during such Military Service.

Regtl. No. 51917 Rank Sergt.
Surname (block letters) NICKERSON
Christian Names in full George William
Regt. Unit

1. Regimental Employment.
Nature of. Period.
(a) From Feby 1919 To May 1919
(b) " "
(c)
(d) " "

*2. Trade or calling before Enlistment (as shown in A. B. 64).
Clerk.

3. Courses of Instruction and Courses in Active Service Army Schools, and certificates, if any.
(a) Army Accounts
(b) London School of Economics
(c) Kingsway W.C.
(d)

*The trade or calling must be filled in by the O.C. Unit from the Appendix to Special Army Order No. 6, of 21st October, 1918 (329 of November, 1918).

[P.T.O.

4. Military qualifications as shewn in A. B. 64.

5. Special Remarks as to qualifications, work done, or skill acquired during service with the Colours. This is required as a help in finding civil employment.

Soldier's Signature (For identification purposes)
Signed (Rank)
Commanding (Unit)

NOTES.—The object of this certificate is to assist the soldier in obtaining employment on his return to civil life. The form will be completed as soon as possible in accordance with Demobilization Regulations.

As soon as signed and completed it will be given to the soldier concerned and will remain his property. He should receive it as early as is compatible with making the necessary references in order that he can either send it home or keep it in his possession.

One form will be issued to each man, and no duplicate can ever be issued.

Figure 151 Certification of Employment during the war

By the 1939 Census, the family were resident at "Emoclew", Lychgate Lane, Burbage, and George is employed as an Assistant Accountant with Hinckley Urban District Council and is also a member of the Home Guard.

In WW2, George joined the Royal Air Force and on 1st August 1941 *The London Gazette* confirmed his promotion to "Acting Pilot Officer on Probation".

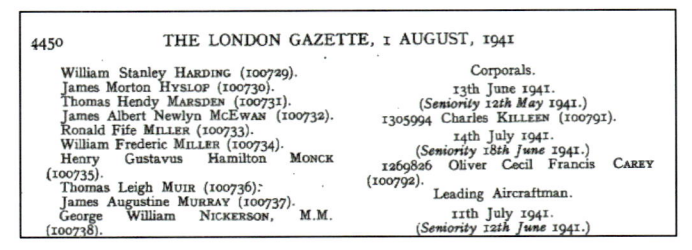

Figure 152 London Gazette 1st August 1941

George was promoted to "Pilot Officer on Probation" as published in *The London Gazette* of 5th September 1941.

After six months service he was drafted to the British Flying Training School in Florida, USA, where he served as Administrative Officer and rose to the rank of Flight Lieutenant.

George developed a malignant lung condition and died suddenly on 31st July 1943 and was buried in Montgomery (Oakwood) Cemetery Annex, Alabama, USA.

Figure 153 FL G W Nickerson

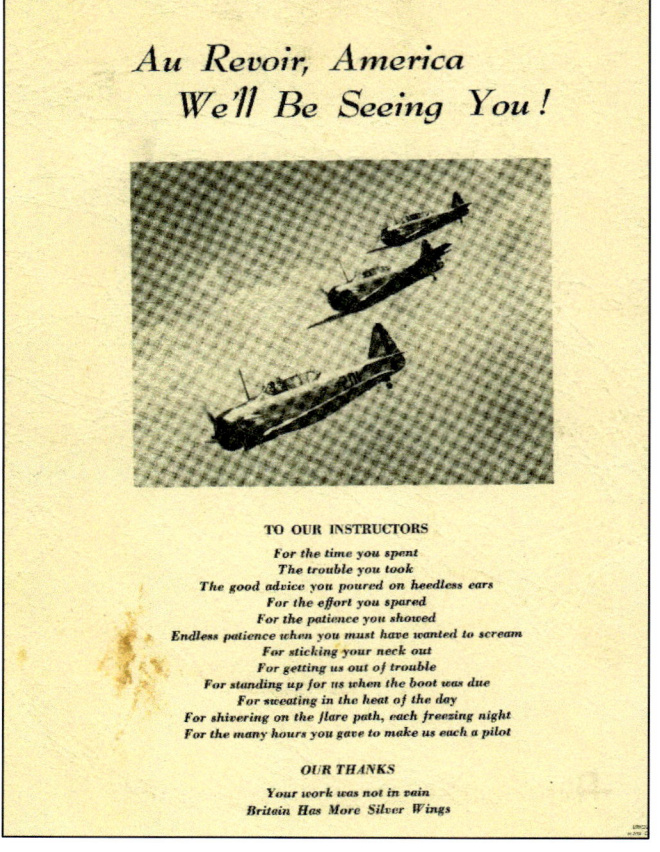

Figure 154 No. 5 British Flying Training School

Montgomery Cemetery

Montgomery (Oakwood) Cemetery Annexe contains 78 Commonwealth burials of the Second World War, all airmen who died while training in Alabama under the British Commonwealth Air Training Plan. There are also 20 French war graves in the cemetery and two non-war burials.

Located in the Oakwood Cemetery Annex, there is a plaque that signifies the burials of 78 officers and men of the British Royal Air Force and a granite cross among the graves. The monument was erected to honour the RAF officers and men whom lost their lives while training during World War II in Montgomery, Alabama.

Figure 155 Montgomery Cemetery, Alabama

Figure 156 Montgomery Cemetery, Alabama

Right: Figure 157 F/L George William Nickerson MM Gravestone

BURBAGE MEMORIAL SERVICE TO F/LT. G. W. NICKERSON

A memorial service was held on Sunday last at St. Catherine's Church, Burbage, in remembrance of F.-Lt. G. W. Nickerson, M.M., who died in the General Hospital at Atlanta City, U.S.A. Ft.-Lt. Nickerson was well known in the district and was formerly in Mr. T. Flavell's office and later with the Hinckley Urban District Council as Rates Clerk.

He was one of the first to join up in the L.D.V., which later became the Home Guard. He was with No. 1 Platoon as second officer and later became O.C. H.Q. Platoon, being very respected in both.

He joined the R.A.F.V.R. about two years ago and after six months in this country was drafted to a training school in Florida, U.S.A., where he was on the Administrative Staff.

The service was conducted by the Rev. R. D. H. Pughe and was attended by Mrs. G. W. Nickerson and his only son, Clifford, who is training as an officer in the R.A.F., and many relatives and friends. The Burbage (No. 1) Platoon Home Guard paraded under Lt. A. Harding and the H.Q. Company under Lt. Whitmore. "A" (Hinckley) Company was also represented by Capt. E. St. J. Makin and C.S.M. Sale. The British Legion, of which he was at one time the Secretary, was also represented and many of his workmates from the Hinckley Urban District Council office. Prayers were said and the Rector paid high tribute to his memory.

Figure 158 Hinckley Times 13th August 1943

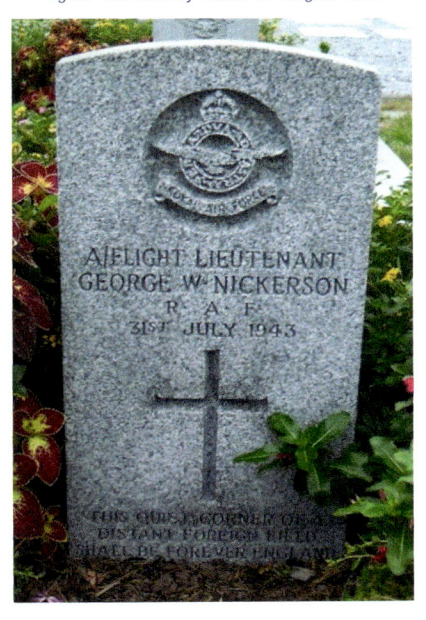

Figure 159 Front row – 4th from left - Flight Lieutenant George William Nickerson

PRIVATE FRANCIS PRITCHARD

Service Number: 5254399
Enlisted: 14th Battalion Sherwood Foresters
Born: 8th March 1918
Died: 6th September 1944, Aged 26
Memorials: Coriano Ridge War Cemetery, Italy
Plot 5, Row D, Grave 1
St Catherine's Church Memorial
Burbage War Memorial

Francis Pritchard was born on 8th March 1918, the eldest son of Harry Frank and Lillian Pritchard of Coventry. At the time of the 1939 census, Francis, his parents and elder sister Doris were living at 24 Colchester Street, Coventry. His father was a Tool Room Foreman and ARP Warden, and Francis was employed as a Bakers Roundsman.

At some point after 1939 the family have moved to "Wymering", Lutterworth Road, Burbage. Here they were recorded on the electoral roll for 1948 and the address is also confirmed by his father's probate record of 1949.

> PRITCHARD Harry Frank of Wymering Lutterworth-road Burbage **Leicestershire** died 8 August 1949 at 93 Bulwer-road Coventry Administration **London** 8 October to Lily Pritchard widow. Effects £329 4s. 3d.

Figure 160 Probate Record 1919

In 1944, Francis married Doris Kimpton of Hertford.

Francis joined the military and was attached to the 14th Battalion of the Sherwood Foresters (Nottingham and Derbyshire Regiment). He was killed on the Allies' initial attempt to take Coriano Ridge in Italy from the Germans on 6th September 1944.

Doris returned to her parents and in the 3rd quarter 1946 remarried in Hertford.

> PRITCHARD, Pte. FRANCIS, 5254399. 14th Bn. The Sherwood Foresters (Notts. and Derby Regt.). 6th September, 1944. Age 26. Son of Harry and Lilian Pritchard; husband of Doris Mary Pritchard, of Hertford. V, D, 1.

Figure 161 Grave Registration

Invasion of Italy

On 3rd September 1943 the Allies invaded the Italian mainland, the invasion coinciding with an armistice made with the Italians who then re-entered the war on the Allied side.

Following the fall of Rome to the Allies in June 1944, the German retreat became ordered and successive stands were made on a series of defensive lines. In the northern Apennine mountains, the last of these, the Gothic Line, was breached by the Allies during the Autumn campaign and the front inched forward as far as Ravenna in the Adriatic sector, but with divisions transferred to support the new offensive in France, and the Germans dug in to a number of key defensive positions, the advance stalled as winter set in.

Coriano Ridge was the last important ridge in the way of the Allied advance in the Adriatic sector in the autumn of 1944. Its capture was the key to Rimini and eventually to the River Po. German parachute and panzer troops, aided by bad weather, resisted all attacks on their positions between 4th and 12th September 1944.

On the night of 12th September, the Eighth Army reopened its attack on the Ridge, with the 1st British and 5th Canadian Armoured Divisions. This attack was successful in taking the Ridge, but marked the beginning of a week of the heaviest fighting experienced since Cassino in May, with daily losses for the Eighth Army of some 150 killed.

The site for the cemetery was selected in April 1945 and was created from graves brought in from the surrounding battlefields. Coriano Ridge War Cemetery contains 1,939 Commonwealth burials of the Second World War.

Figure 162 Coriano Ridge War Cemetery, Italy

MR SYDNEY HARRY SHAW

Enlisted: National Fire Service
Born: 16th August 1892, Desford
Died: 9th April 1941, Aged 47
Memorials: London Road Cemetery, Coventry
Mass Grave for the Coventry Blitz
Burbage War Memorial
St Catherine's Church Memorial

Sydney Harry Shaw was born on 16th August 1892, the fourth of 7 children of George and Annie Shaw of Desford. At the time of the 1911 census, Sydney was employed as a Pony Driver at Desford Colliery.

On 27th December 1913, Sydney married Elizabeth Barrett of Burbage and by the time of the 1939 census, Syndey was employed as a Hosiery Maker and lived at 21 Flamville Road with his wife and 9 of their 12 children. Sydney fought in WW1, during this war he received a shrapnel injury to his ankle.

Sydney was employed at a factory in Ansty, near Coventry, which assembled mosquito aircraft for the war effort, and was for many years a 'Rolls Royce' establishment. In addition to his duties at the factory, he was also a part-time Fireman.

These factories produced aircraft under the governments "shadow scheme" using technology transfer and the manufacturing facilities of the motor industry to produce aircraft for the war effort.

In April 1941, whilst working at Ansty, Sydney was injured when a propeller fell onto him, during maintenance works. He was taken to hospital and his wife visited him that evening and she was informed that he needed to stay at the hospital and she told him she would visit the next day. That night, 9th April, the Coventry & Warwickshire Hospital was bombed, during a Coventry bomber attack on the city. Sydney, along with a number of doctors and nurses, was killed in the raid.

Sydney was laid to rest in a mass grave at London Road Cemetery, Coventry, one of the 808 people who were killed in the bombings during November 1940 and April 1941

Figure 163 Mass Grave at London Road Cemetery, Coventry

Figure 164 The Civilian Monument at London Road, Cemetery

Figure 165 Mass Grave in London Road Cemetery

SHAW, SYDNEY HARRY, age 47. Husband of Elizabeth Shaw, of 21 Flamville Road, Burbage, Leicestershire. 9 April 1941, at Coventry and Warwickshire Hospital.

Figure 166 Record of Civilian War Dead

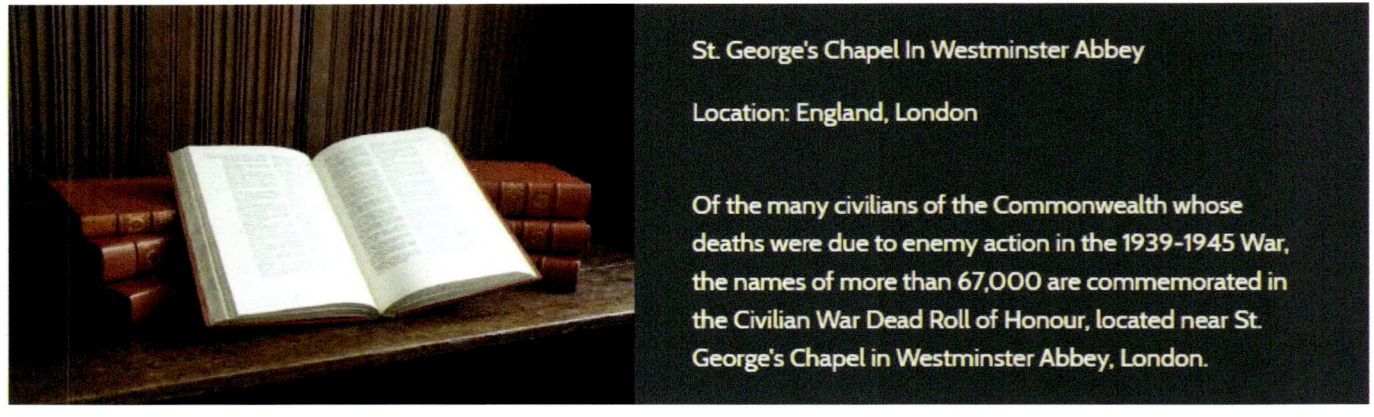

St. George's Chapel In Westminster Abbey

Location: England, London

Of the many civilians of the Commonwealth whose deaths were due to enemy action in the 1939-1945 War, the names of more than 67,000 are commemorated in the Civilian War Dead Roll of Honour, located near St. George's Chapel in Westminster Abbey, London.

Figure 167 Civilian War Dead

Figure 168 De Havilland Mosquito Assembly – Coventry

SARGEANT GEORGE HENRY SMITH

Service Number: 4855491

Enlisted: Leicestershire Regiment and later assigned to the 2nd Battalion of the Royal Berkshire Regiment

Born Tuesday 1st December 1908

Died Sunday 18th March 1945, Aged 36

Memorials: Rangoon Memorial, East Yangon Region, Myanmar. Face 15

Burbage War Memorial

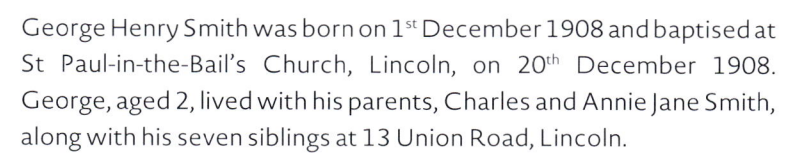

George Henry Smith was born on 1st December 1908 and baptised at St Paul-in-the-Bail's Church, Lincoln, on 20th December 1908. George, aged 2, lived with his parents, Charles and Annie Jane Smith, along with his seven siblings at 13 Union Road, Lincoln.

Figure 169 13 Union Road, Lincoln

Following his education, George worked as a labourer until enlisting with the Leicestershire Regiment on 29th August 1929. Serving as a Private, he was stationed in India for six years between 1930 and 1937, during which time he trained as a Nursing Orderly. He was transferred to the Army Reserves on 28th July 1937.

George met a local Burbage girl, Kathleen Meeks, and they married at Hinckley Registry Office on 3rd August 1940. They established their home at 7 Flamville Road, Burbage. Kathleen was the daughter of Archibald and Mabel Ellen Meeks.

Figure 170 George & Kathleen Smith

Even before the declaration of war on 3rd September 1939, George had already been mobilised as a reservist at Leicester on 1st September. He received his first posting on 30th March 1940 and was promoted to Corporal in 1941. Between 1940 and 1943, he was granted several periods of leave, with warrants to travel home. In December 1943, George was posted to India, arriving in Bombay on 23rd January 1944. Soon after his arrival, he was transferred to the 2nd Battalion of the Royal Berkshire Regiment and promoted to Sergeant that same year.

Figure 171 George Smith (during the time he held the rank of Corporal)

In July 1944, Kathleen gave birth to their daughter, who continues to reside in Burbage. Sadly, George never had the chance to meet his young child, as he was killed in March the following year.

George was initially reported missing, and it was not until January 1946 that he was finally confirmed as "killed in action" on 18th March 1945, aged 36, whilst serving in Burma. George is commemorated on the Rangoon Memorial in Burma. However, he was not originally honoured on any UK War Memorial, an omission corrected in 2024 when his name was added to the fallen of WW2 on the Burbage War Memorial.

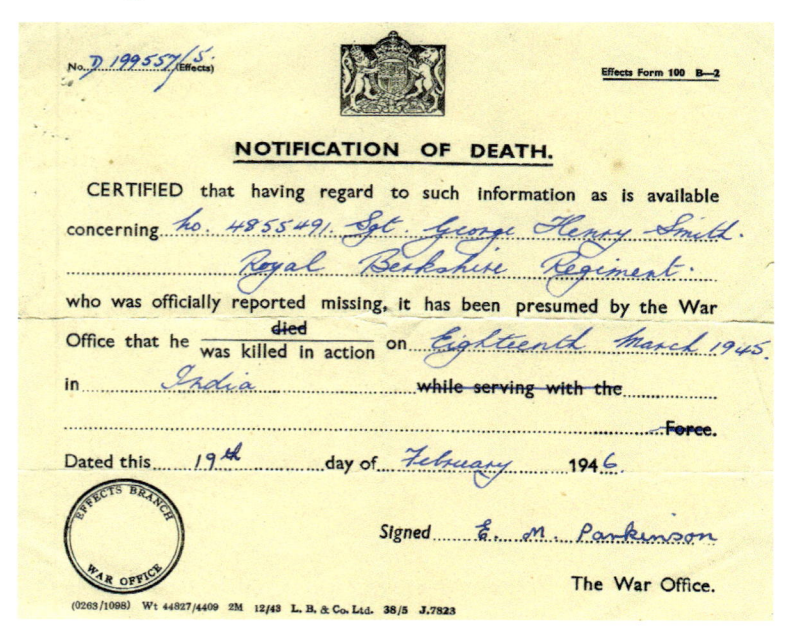

Figure 172 Notification of Death

BURBAGE SERGEANT PRESUMED DEAD

Sergt. George Smith

News has been received by Mrs. Kathleen Smith, of 7 Flamville Road, Burbage, that her husband, Sergt. George H. Smith, who was reported missing in Burma on March 18th, 1945, is now presumed dead.

Sgt. Smith, a regular soldier, had completed his army service nine months before the war broke out, but he was recalled to the colours, going overseas two years last December. He was in the 19th Division. Altogether Sgt. Smith had 17 years army service to his credit. He leaves a widow and an eighteen months old daughter whom he had never seen. Sgt. Smith belonged to a Lincolnshire family.

Figure 173 Hinckley Times 1st February 1946.

THE FALLEN

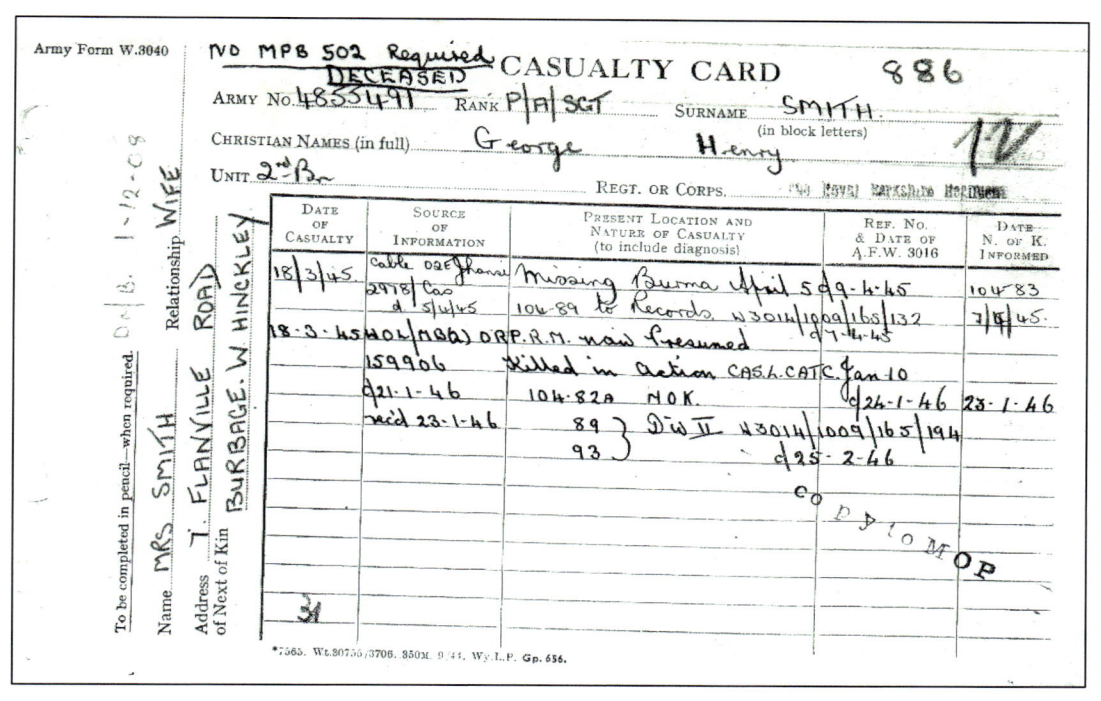

Figure 174 Casualty Record

Figure 175 Rangoon Memorial

BUCKINGHAM PALACE

The Queen and I offer you our heartfelt sympathy in your great sorrow.

We pray that your country's gratitude for a life so nobly given in its service may bring you some measure of consolation.

George R.I.

Figure 176 Buckingham Palace letter of Consolation

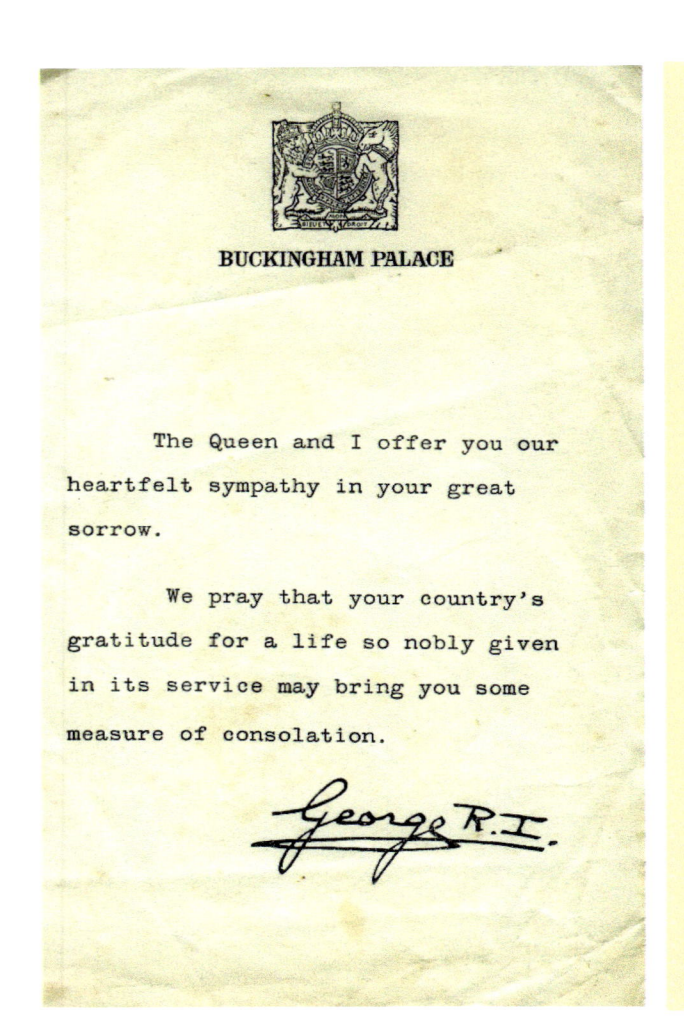

This scroll commemorates

Serjeant G. H. Smith
Royal Berkshire Regiment

held in honour as one who served King and Country in the world war of 1939-1945 and gave his life to save mankind from tyranny. May his sacrifice help to bring the peace and freedom for which he died.

Figure 177 Scroll of honour

LIEUTENANT THOMAS FRANK SMITH

Service Number: 210423
Enlisted: 51st Medium Regiment, Royal Artillery
Born: 21st September 1905
Died: 12th May 1943, Aged 37
Memorials: Enfidaville War Cemetery, Tunisia
Plot 4, Row C, Grave 5
St Catherine's Church Memorial
Burbage War Memorial
Hinckley Grammar School Memorial

Thomas Frank Smith was born on 21st September 1905, the eldest son of Police Superintendent Frederic George and May Smith of the Police Station, Stockwell Head, Hinckley. Thomas attended the Hinckley Grammar School.

The 1939 Census shows Thomas living at 72 Sketchley Road, Burbage with his wife Daisy May and his son. He was employed as the Manager of a Wine & Spirits Merchant and also served as an Air Raid Warden for Hinckley Urban District Council.

Thomas was a Lieutenant with the 51st Medium Regiment of the Royal Artillery. In the autumn of 1942, 51st Medium Regiment embarked at Liverpool and arrived in Egypt in October to join Middle East Forces (MEF) whose role was to defend British interests in the Middle East. In January 1943 the MEF were re-equipped with the 4.5-inch gun and moved up to join the Eighth Army. As part of 5th Army Group Royal Artillery (AGRA) the MEF took part in the battles of the Mareth Line, Wadi Akarit and Enfidaville in March and April 1943.

Sadly, Thomas was killed on 12th May 1943 during this pivotal battle, which resulted in significant casualties. Thomas is interred at Enfidaville War Cemetery, where 1,551 servicemen are buried.

The Battle of Enfidaville

The fighting around Enfidaville in North Africa during April and May 1943 was a critical chapter in the final stages of the Tunisian Campaign. As Allied forces pressed forward to eliminate Axis presence in Tunisia, Enfidaville became a key defensive stronghold for German and Italian forces under General Giovanni Messe, owing to its challenging mountainous terrain and fortified positions.

On 19th April 1943, the British Eighth Army, led by General Montgomery, launched its initial assault on Enfidaville. Determined to break through Axis defences, Allied troops faced fierce resistance. One of the most intense battles occurred on 20th/21st April, when Allied forces captured the vital hilltop village of Takrouna after brutal combat. Despite this success, the Axis defenders skilfully used minefields, artillery, and machine-gun nests to slow the Allied advance.

By 29th April, the Eighth Army was forced to pause its offensive due to the difficult terrain and strong enemy fortifications. However, the strategic importance of Enfidaville kept it in focus as the Allies planned their next moves.

The tide turned on May 6 with the launch of Operation Vulcan, a large-scale Allied offensive aimed at crushing the remaining Axis forces in Tunisia. This was followed by Operation Strike on 11th May, which delivered the final blow to Axis defensive lines. With their positions overwhelmed and supply lines severed, Axis troops in Enfidaville, along with other strongholds in Tunisia, surrendered on 13th May 1943.

The fall of Enfidaville marked the end of the North African Campaign, leading to the capture of over 275,000 Axis soldiers and paving the way for the Allied invasion of Sicily and the subsequent Italian Campaign.

Figure 178 4.5-inch gun

Figure 179 Enfidaville War Cemetery, Tunisia

Figure 180 Gravestone Enfidaville War Cemetery, Tunisia

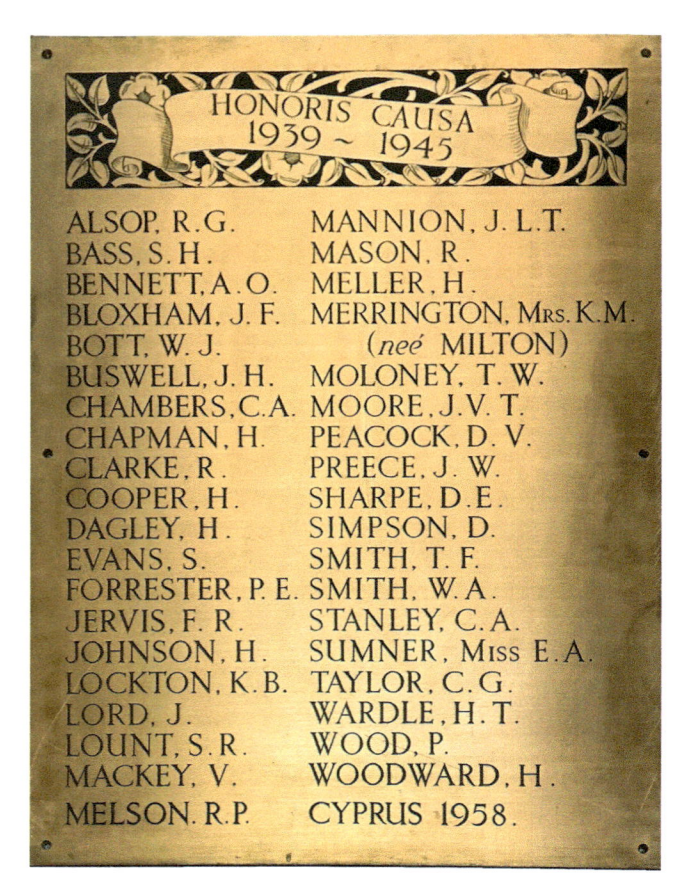

HONORIS CAUSA 1939 ~ 1945

ALSOP, R.G.	MANNION, J.L.T.
BASS, S.H.	MASON, R.
BENNETT, A.O.	MELLER, H.
BLOXHAM, J.F.	MERRINGTON, Mrs. K.M.
BOTT, W.J.	(neé MILTON)
BUSWELL, J.H.	MOLONEY, T.W.
CHAMBERS, C.A.	MOORE, J.V.T.
CHAPMAN, H.	PEACOCK, D.V.
CLARKE, R.	PREECE, J.W.
COOPER, H.	SHARPE, D.E.
DAGLEY, H.	SIMPSON, D.
EVANS, S.	SMITH, T.F.
FORRESTER, P.E.	SMITH, W.A.
JERVIS, F.R.	STANLEY, C.A.
JOHNSON, H.	SUMNER, Miss E.A.
LOCKTON, K.B.	TAYLOR, C.G.
LORD, J.	WARDLE, H.T.
LOUNT, S.R.	WOOD, P.
MACKEY, V.	WOODWARD, H.
MELSON, R.P.	CYPRUS 1958

Figure 181 Hinckley Grammar School Memorial

LIEUT. TOM F. SMITH KILLED IN TUNISIA

Lieut. T. F. Smith

Lieut. Tom F. Smith, eldest son of the late Supt. F. G. Smith, police chief of the Bosworth Division, and Mrs. Smith, was killed while serving with the R.A. in the last of the fighting in Tunisia. A letter from the deceased's Colonel conveyed the sad news to the widow, who resides in Sketchley Road, Burbage.

Lieut. Smith had been in the Royal Artillery for three years. He leaves a widow and a little boy.

Before joining up he was in the employ of Messrs. J. C. Bonsir and Co., Castle Street.

Right: Figure 182 Hinckley Times 4th June 1943

TROOPER BERT EDWARD THATCHER

Service Number: 551639
Enlisted: 4th Queen's Own Hussars
Royal Armoured Corps
Born: 13th August 1912
Died: 9th February 1945, Aged 33
Memorials: Klagenfurt Commonwealth War Cemetery, Austria
Plot 2, Row E, Grave 1.
Burbage War Memorial

Bert Edward Thatcher was born in Stoke, Coventry, the son of Bertie Edward and Kate Thatcher of 85 Chandos Street. By the time Bert was ten they had moved to Burbage, where Bert and his elder sister Florence May attended the National School.

Bert was a reservist and had six years' service, four and a half of which had been abroad. When war was declared in September 1939, Bert had been at home for 2 years, working for Hinckley Urban District Council and was living with his parents at 42 Freemans Lane, Burbage.

He was taken prisoner in Greece in April 1941 and died whilst held prisoner by the German army, on 9th February 1945. Bert is buried at Klagenfurt Commonwealth War Cemetery, Austria.

Records indicate that Bert was held prisoner at Stalag 344 at Lambinowice, Poland and most probably died whilst being marched to Germany. In January 1945, the Soviet Army advanced into Poland and the German High Command made the decision to evacuate the POW camps to prevent the liberation of the prisoners by the Russians. Many of the prisoners were marched westward in groups of 200 to 300 in the so-called Long March or Death March (see page 91). Many of them died from the bitter cold and exhaustion.

Austria was annexed by Germany in March 1938. Many labour, prisoner-of-war and concentration camps were established there. The principal POW camps were at Döllersheim, Gneixendorf, Kaisersteinbruch, Lienz, Spittal an der Drau, Wolfsberg and Graz. Commonwealth war dead buried in Austria were mainly servicemen who died in these camps in captivity, airmen who were shot down or crashed while flying over the country and those who died while serving with the army of occupation after the war. Klagenfurt, the only Commonwealth war cemetery in Austria, was begun in June 1945 by the British occupying forces, who moved graves into it from all over the country. It now contains 589 Commonwealth burials of the Second World War.

TROOPER B. E. THATCHER

Trooper Bert E. Thatcher, of The Hussars, eldest son of Mr. and Mrs. Thatcher, of 42, Freeman's Lane, Burbage, has been reported missing since April 28th, while serving with H.M. forces in the Middle East.

Trooper Thatcher, who was 29 years of age, had served ten years in the Hussars, and was, for 4½ years of peace time in Eqypt. He had been decorated for distinction while serving in Palestine.

Up to the outbreak of war he was employed as a lorry driver by the Hinckley Urban District Council.

Figure 183 Hinckley Times Report 13th June 1941

Trooper B. E. Thatcher a Prisoner of War

A communication from the Red Cross intimating that Trooper B. E. Thatcher, of The Hussars, is a prisoner of war at a camp in Germany, has been received by his mother, Mrs. Thatcher, of 42, Freeman's Lane, Burbage.

This was the first news Mrs. Thatcher had received of her eldest son since he was reported missing on April 28th, and her anxiety during the intervening months can be well imagined. However, news of his safety has come as a great relief to his parents and to his many friends in the Hinckley locality. He was reported missing on April 28th, while serving with the Forces in the Middle East.

Thatcher, who is 29 years of age, had served for ten years in the Hussars, and was for 4½ years of peace time in Egypt. He was decorated for distinction while serving in Palestine. Before the outbreak of war he was employed as a lorry driver by the Hinckley Urban District Council.

TROOPER. B. E THATCHER

Figure 184 *Hinckley Times 29 August 1941*

Figure 185 Klagenfurt Commonwealth War Cemetery, Austria

Figure 186 Trooper Bert Edward Thatcher Gravestone

TROOPER BERT THATCHER DIES IN GERMANY

Trooper Bert Thatcher

Mr. and Mrs. B. Thatcher, of 42, Freeman's Lane, Burbage, have received the sad news that their eldest son, Tpr. Bert Thatcher, of the 4th Hussars, died on February 9th last while a prisoner of war in German hands.

Tpr. Thatcher was a reservist and had only been home two years, after six years service, including four and a half years abroad, when he was re-called on the outbreak of war.

He was taken prisoner in Greece in April, 1941.

Before the war he was employed as a driver by the Hinckley Urban District Council.

Figure 187 Hinckley Times 6th July 1945

The Long March

The Long March was during the final months of the Second World War in Europe. About 30,000 Allied PoWs were force-marched westward across Poland and Germany in appalling winter conditions, lasting about four months from January to April 1945. It has been called various names: "The Great March West", "The Long March", "The Long Walk", "The Long Trek", "The Black March", "The Bread March", but most survivors just called it "The March". It has also been called "The Lamsdorf Death March".

As the Soviet army was advancing on Poland, the Nazis made the decision to evacuate the PoW camps to prevent the liberation of the prisoners by the Russians. During this period, also hundreds of thousands of German civilians, most of them women and children, as well as civilians of other nationalities, were making their way westward in the snow and freezing weather and many died. January and February 1945 were among the coldest winter months of the twentieth century, with blizzards and temperatures as low as –25°C (–13°F), even until the middle of March temperatures were well below 0°F (–18°C). Most of the PoWs were ill-prepared for the evacuation, having suffered years of poor rations and wearing clothing ill-suited to the appalling winter conditions.

Each Stalag was responsible for co-ordinating the movement of POW at the outlying labour camps as well as those at the main camp. In the case of Stalag 344 Lamsdorf (formerly Stalag VIII-B) they took a northerly route via Dresden.

www.lamsdorf.com

GUNNER JEFFREY TITE

Service Number: 956443
Enlisted: Bedfordshire Yeomanry, December 1939
Born: 26th July 1919
Died: 22nd September 1943, Aged 24
Memorials: Chungkai War Cemetery, Thailand, Plot 2, Row N, Grave 1
St Catherine's Church Memorial,
Congregational Church Memorial,
Burbage War Memorial

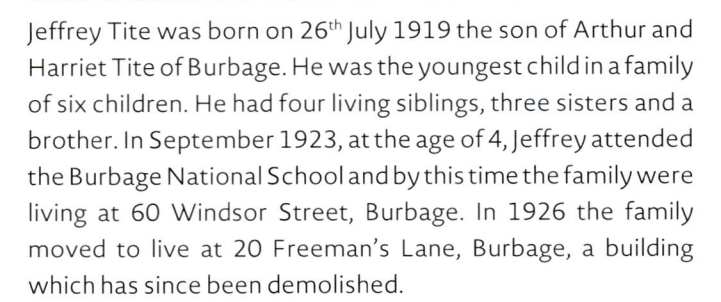

Jeffrey Tite was born on 26th July 1919 the son of Arthur and Harriet Tite of Burbage. He was the youngest child in a family of six children. He had four living siblings, three sisters and a brother. In September 1923, at the age of 4, Jeffrey attended the Burbage National School and by this time the family were living at 60 Windsor Street, Burbage. In 1926 the family moved to live at 20 Freeman's Lane, Burbage, a building which has since been demolished.

Figure 188 Jeffrey Tite (front)

Prior to joining the Bedfordshire Yeomanry in 1939, Jeffrey was employed as a gardener for Mr W Flavell of The Lodge, Lutterworth Road, Burbage.

Jeffery Tite, along with another Burbage casualty Harry Dobson, joined the 148th (The Bedfordshire Yeomanry) Field Regiment, Royal Artillery towards the end of 1939, after war broke.

Over the next three years, the two friends were transported worldwide and eventually became prisoners of war in Thailand, forced to build the Thailand–Burma Railway.

Their story, together with that of Harold Letts of Burbage, is told on page 100.

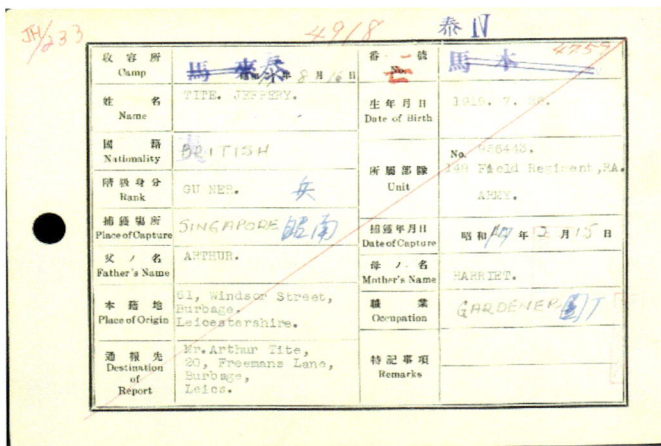

Figure 189 Prisoner of War Record

Jeffrey was forced to labour on the railway construction until the time of his death on 22nd September 1943 from malnutrition. In was in July 1945 that his mother, Mrs A Tite received news of Jeffery's death the previous September.

Gunner J. Tite

Mrs. A. Tite, of 20, Freeman's Lane, Burbage, has received news that her son, Gunner Jeffrey Tite, a prisoner of war in Japanese hands, died on September 22nd, 1943, from avitaminosis. He was 24 at the time of his death.

Gunner Tite, who joined the Army in 1939, was taken prisoner when Singapore fell. Before the war he was employed as a gardener by Mr. W. Flavell, of Lutterworth Road, Burbage.

Figure 190 Hinckley Times 6th July 1945

The Fallen

THAILAND-BURMA RAILWAY CENTRE
POW DEATH RECORD

SERVICE No.	956443
RANK	Gunner
SURNAME	TITE
OTHER NAMES	JEFFERY
NATIONALITY	British
UNIT	148 (The Bedfordshire Yeomanry) Field Regiment, Royal Artillery.
FORCE (GROUP)	xxx
WORK AREAS	xxx
DATE OF DEATH	22/09/1943
PLACE OF DEATH	Chungkai Camp
FIRST BURIED	Chungkai New Cemetery, Grave No. 0499
CAUSE OF DEATH	Polyavitaminosis, Septic Renphyces
AGE	23
NEXT OF KIN	Arthur and Harriett Tite, of Burbage, Leicestershire.
CEMETERY (NOW)	Chungkai
GRAVE No.	2. N. 01

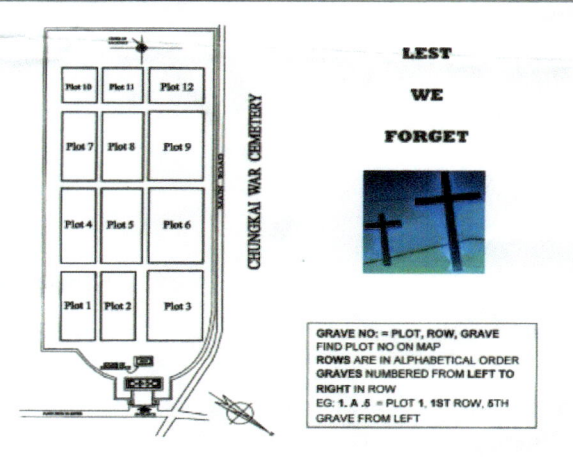

LEST WE FORGET

GRAVE NO: = PLOT, ROW, GRAVE
FIND PLOT NO ON MAP
ROWS ARE IN ALPHABETICAL ORDER
GRAVES NUMBERED FROM LEFT TO RIGHT IN ROW
EG: 1. A .5 = PLOT 1, 1ST ROW, 5TH GRAVE FROM LEFT

Figure 191 Thailand-Burma Railway Centre, POW Death Record

Figure 192 Gunner Jeffrey Tite (1919 – 1943)

Figure 193 Jeffrey Tite, Plot 2, Row N, Grave 1

Figure 194 Chungkai War Cemetery, Thailand

FUSILIER WALTER WHITE

Service Number: 6982018
Enlisted: 1st Battalion Royal Inniskilling Regiment
Born: 13th April 1920, Basford, Nottinghamshire
Died: 26th April 1943 Calcutta, India, Aged 23
Memorials:
Bhowanipore Cemetery, Calcutta, India
Plot O, Row G, Grave 35
Burbage War Memorial
St Catherine's Church Memorial

Walter White was born on 13th April 1920, the son of Annie Maria White of Calverton, Nottinghamshire. Annie married Bertie Strutt in the 2nd quarter of 1921 in Nottinghamshire and by the time of the 1939 Census they were living at 56 Sapcote Road, Burbage. Bertie Strutt was a bus driver; Annie was a mender for a hosiery manufacturer and Walter was employed as a joiner's labourer.

During World War II, Walter was a Fusilier with the 1st Battalion Royal Inniskilling Regiment who were stationed in India. In 1942, the First Battalion was flown to Burma to help stem the Japanese advance and in 1943 took part in the operations in the Arakan Peninsula.

In January 1942, the army of Imperial Japan invaded the British possession of Burma. The British and British Indian army forces were out flanked, defeated and were forced to evacuate Burma. The Inniskillings had been flown into Burma as part of an unsuccessful attempt to create a defensive line north of Rangoon. It failed, and the order to evacuate Burma was given and India itself was now threatened.

In 1943, there was another unsuccessful campaign to halt the advance of the Japanese army. The intention of the campaign was to attack the left flank (see map on opposite page) of the Japanese forces threatening India[1]. This was to be carried out by 14th Indian Division, commanded by Major General W L Lloyd.

In this Division were the Inniskillings of the 47th Infantry Brigade, with two other battalions, the 1st and 5th Battalions, together with the 7th Rajput and 8th Punjab Regiments..

By 6th April, a disorderly withdrawal was now in progress across jungle covered hills, with speed reduced to ½ mile per hour. When darkness fell, direction was kept by touch only. The Battalion had to split into small forces and had to hide up during the day to avoid Japanese patrols. The parties made for the beach south of Indin. Casualties were high from Japanese ambushes and prisoners were taken. The remains of the Battalion were moved to staging camps and then were transported by motor transport to the north across the border into India.

It is likely that Walter was injured during this campaign, he died on 26th April 1943 and is buried in Bhowanipore Cemetery, Calcutta, India.

Figure 195 Walter White

---

[1] http://www.inniskillingsmuseum.com/the-inniskillings-in-burma-january-april-1943/

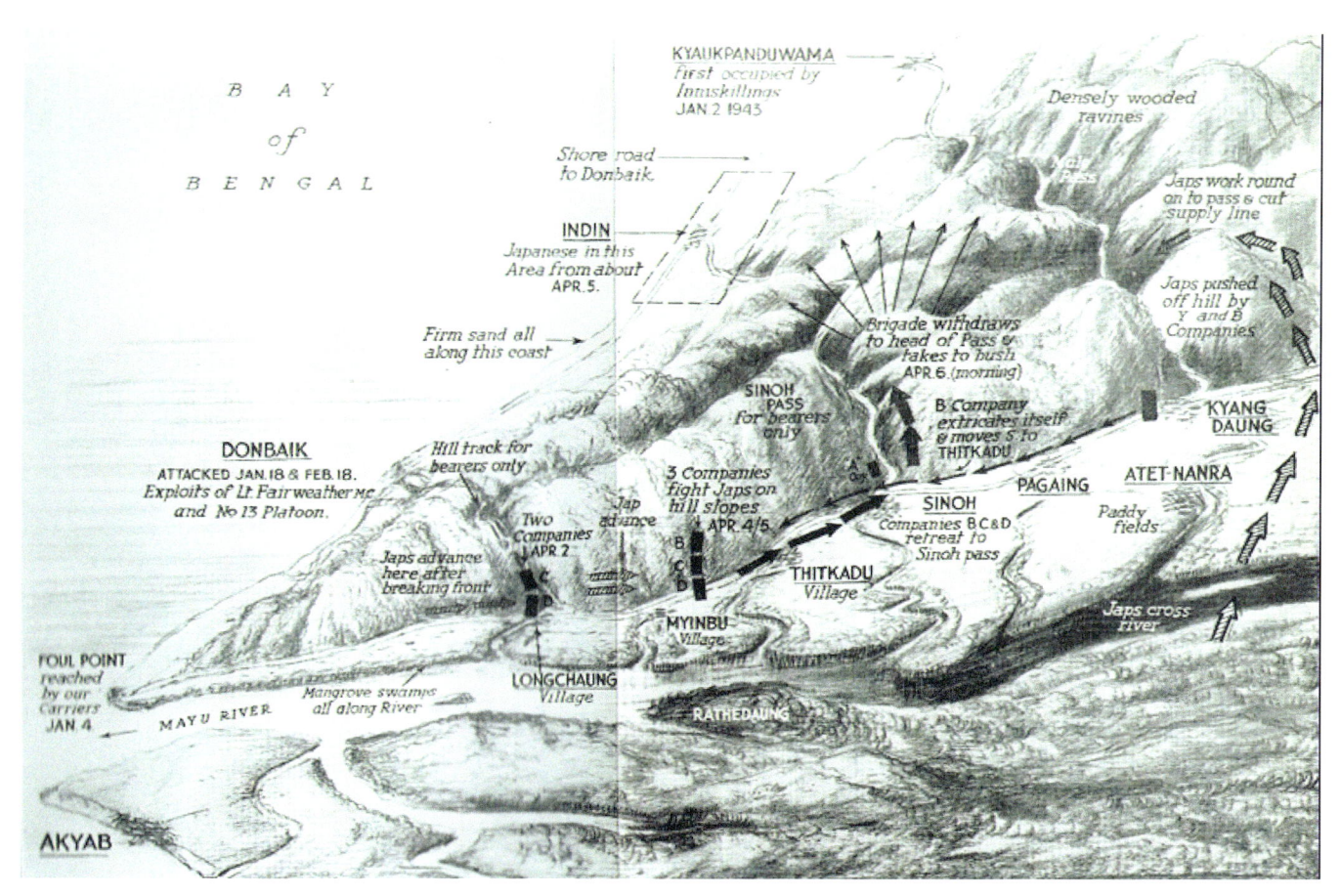

Figure 196 Arakan Peninsula

Figure 197 Bhowanipore Cemetery, Calcutta, India

Figure 198 Bhowanipore Cemetery, Calcutta, India

CORPORAL DOUGLAS ARTHUR WOOD

Service Number: 5051796
Enlisted: 1st Battalion Northamptonshire Regiment
Born: 28th November 1917
Died: 22nd February 1945, Aged 27
Memorials: Taukkyan War Cemetery, Myanmar, Burma
Plot 27, Row H, Collective Grave 1-17
Burbage War Memorial
Wesleyan Memorial

Douglas Wood was born towards the end of WW1 in 1917. In 1939, at the age of 21, he married local girl Kate Hill at the Wesleyan Church in Burbage. Her parents were stewards at the Constitutional Club.

Figure 199 Wedding of Douglas Wood and Kate Hill

Kate was a nursing auxiliary at Hinckley Hospital and Douglas worked at the Sketchley Dye Works. Just eight months after their wedding Douglas was called up in 1940. After two years' service at various postings, Douglas was sent out east in 1942. In late 1944 and early 1945, the Allied Army launched offensives into Burma intending to recover the country, including Rangoon, the capital, from the Japanese before the onset of the monsoon in May.

The Japanese Burma Area Army attempted to forestall the main Allied attack on the centre of the country by withdrawing their troops behind the Irrawaddy River. They hoped the Allies lines of communications would be overstretched trying to cross this obstacle. However, the advancing British 14th Army switched its axis of advance to outflank the main Japanese armies.

During February and March, the 14th Army secured bridgeheads across the Irrawaddy on a broad front. On 1st March units of the British IV corps captured the supply centre of Meiktila throwing the Japanese into disarray and turning the tide of the war in Burma.

Unfortunately, Douglas did not live to see this Allied advance, as he was shot walking through the jungle by a Japanese sniper and killed instantly on 22nd February 1945. Douglas was buried at the largest of the three war cemeteries, Taukkyan in Burma. A picture of the cemetery is shown on page 43.

CORPL. W. D. WOOD KILLED IN BURMA

Corporal D. Wood

Corporal Douglas Wood, whose wife, formerly Miss Kate Hill, lives at "Deanwood," Coventry Road, Burbage, and who is a son of Mrs. and the late Mr. Albert Wood, of Hinckley, has been killed in action in Burma. His wife received official notification of his death last Saturday. He was serving with another Burbage fellow who actually saw Wood fall. He was 27 years of age and was employed at Sketchley Dye Works before joining the Army nearly five years ago, three years having been spent in the Eastern theatre of war.

Figure 200 Hinckley Times 16th March 1945

After the war, in 1946, Kate, his widow, married Fred Chandler, a fellow soldier who had served alongside Douglas in Burma when he was killed. They had two sons, naming their eldest Douglas in his memory.

Figure 201 Taukkyan War Cemetery, Plot 27, Row H, Collective Grave 1-17

In 1985, Kate was selected along with a hundred other war widows and veterans to tour around Singapore and Burma and she visited many of the war cemeteries. The visit was organised by the Royal British Legion.

Some forty years after he had died Kate finally visited her husband's grave where she saw the inscription she had chosen for his stone 'Worthy of everlasting remembrance'.

In 1996, the Burbage War Memorial Garden was replanted and Kate contributed to the fund. In 1999, the actual memorial was renovated and new gates were added.

Throughout her long life, Kate never missed a Remembrance Day Service and always laid a wreath. After her death in 2003, the family have carried on this tradition.

A memorial to Douglas originally in the Wesleyan Methodist Church in Burbage is now kept by the family. A large copper plaque attached to the communion table with the names of the four Methodists that were killed in WWII, F Holyoak, H Letts, H Howkins and D Wood. Kate rescued the plaque from a skip in the 1980s when the church was being renovated and it was reinstated in the church in 2004, after the Methodist Church was rebuilt in the 2010s the plaque was again recovered by the family.

Figure 202 Kate Chandler (formerly Mrs Wood)

Figure 203 Wesleyan Methodist Church Memorial

MY PILGRAMAGE TO SINGAPORE AND BURMA by Kate Chandler

We flew out from Brize Norton RAF Station on a Tristar, after spending overnight there, where we were made very welcome, and introduced and mingled with all the war widows, war veterans, British Legion, Medical Staff and the support party, who all made us most welcome and were magnificent in every way.

As it was my first time on a plane, let alone going to the Far East, I was very nervous, but I put my trust in God and the RAF Plane Crew and settled down to enjoy the flight.

We travelled over France, where we had some turbulence over the French Alps, then over Egypt where we had a good view of the River Nile at 35,000 feet up, the Co-Pilot taking a photograph for me from the cockpit.

Afterwards, flying round the coast of India, the Pilot told us we couldn't fly over India as it was an RAF plane.

Our first stop was at Bahrain, where we were allowed off for about 1½ hours. Our next stop was at Bangkok, where the Thailand party disembarked for their pilgrimage; we were allowed off for an hour.

Getting on the plane again, this time for Singapore.

We all disembarked at Singapore and were taken to the "Oberoe Imperial Hotel" which was a lovely Hotel with all modern conveniences.

We stayed at Singapore for 2 days, being taken round the shops, with a tour round the Island and a meal at "Raffles Hotel".

On Friday morning, we were to be up early for "The Burma Party" to be taken to Burma, about two hours flying time. Arriving at Rangoon Airport we had a bumpy descent, as an RAF Tristar had never been to Rangoon before, as it was such a small air field. After an hour or so, we were allowed out of the airport and met by the British Embassy Staff, who took us to our Hotel for our stay in Burma, which was the "Inya Lanke Hotel".

Burma is a very poor country, unlike Singapore, and we were not allowed to stay any longer than 4 days, it being a communist country, and trying to be self-supporting, but the Embassy staff said they were trying to westernize them, but it would take a very long time, as the Burmese were quite content to live like that.

On Saturday we had a Memorial Service at Rangoon War Memorial, where the weather was very hot and sticky, afterwards being taken to HM Consul & Mrs. Smallman's residence for a reception, then on to the Taukkyan War Cemetery (They told us this was the largest cemetery in the Far East) for a private visit, so we could find where our former husband's graves were "War Graves Commission" always at hand to help you.

Such a beautiful cemetery, with shrubs and bushes at each grave, 26,000 in all, with thousands with no names, just "A Soldier, known only to God". I found my former husband's grave (Cpl. D. A. Wood), and placed on it 2 crosses, one for myself and one for my late husband Fred, who I know would have wished it, as he would have been eligible to have gone had he lived, as Fred was along with Doug all the way through the Burma Campaign, and with him when he was killed.

Figure 204 Account of 1985 Pilgrimage to Burma by Kate Chandler – Page 1

Sunday

Today, we had a lie in, Breakfast being 8.30.a.m. and able to choose which place of worship to attend. Four of us went to the British Methodist Church, by special bus, from the Hotel. It was a lovely little church, the service being organised by the Burmese boys and girls, as it was International Youth Year.

After lunch, we were taken again by bus, to the Schwebegon Pagoda where we had to take off our shoes, and walk up 98 steps to get to it. It was like a small village, I understand it was the Burmese religion to give all their money to pay for the gold which over the years is used for keeping the Pagodas in good repair.

In the evening it was our Memorial Service at Rangoon Cathedral, 7.30.p.m. It was filled to overflowing with a lot of Burmese people there, as well as Mr. Michael Hesseltine and all the Heads of State. The service coincided with the service at Burbage Methodist, as we were 8½ hours in front of British time, so now I would like to thank Rev. D. Cooper for remembering me in his prayers on that day.

Monday 11th November

Up at 5.30 a.m. (woken up by Buglers playing Reveille) for our service at Taukkyan War Cemetery at 8 a.m.

This was a lovely service but very emotional, afterwards we were able to place a wreath on our husband's grave with the words ringing in our ears, as the Burma Star War veteran recited the epitaph on the Kohima Memorial

> **When you go home**
> **Tell them of us, and say,**
> **For your Tomorrow, we gave our Today**

So after a sad, but memorable journey and also feeling at peace, knowing now where they are buried, I walk up the steps to the plane for home with the hymn

God moves in a mysterious way
His wonders to perform

And I thank God and all the support staff, for me being well and able to make it such a memorable pilgrimage, one which I shall never ever forget.

Thailand – Burma Railway

Construction of the Burma-Siam railway began in October 1942 and ended in October 1943. Around 60,000 British, Australian, Dutch and American prisoners of war; civilian labourers from Burma, Singapore, Malaya, Java and Thailand, were forced by the Japanese to build a 420 km railway through mountainous jungle. An estimated 13,000 PoWs and 70,000 civilian workers died, among these were three Burbage men, Harry Dobson, Harold Letts and Jeffery Tite. The prisoners of war who were forced to work on the railway called it the Death Railway.

All of these were in Singapore when the British forces were forced to surrender, and Dobson and Tite had a shared journey to Singapore. The following sections recount the journey to Singapore and their experiences as prisoners of war.

Dobson & Tite's Journey to the Far East

In September 1939, the 148th Field Regiment's barracks were in Luton, Bedfordshire. The following information is based on an account by fellow soldier, Kenneth S Burns who was posted to the 148th Field Regiment in 1940, their service career would have taken the following path up to their arrival in Singapore.

In 1940 they trained in Norfolk and they also received field gun training at Larkhill on Salisbury Plain. Later they continued their training in Hawick in the Scottish Borders, then three months in Rochdale, followed by a training camp at Trawsfynydd in what is now Snowdonia National Park and finally, to Monmouth, before going overseas.

On October 30th 1941 they embarked on S.S. Andes, a commandeered passenger liner and by account the whole of the 148th Field Regiment were on this ship including Harry Dobson and Jeffrey Tite. The Andes set sail on 1st November with an escort of three destroyers.

Figure 206 SS Andes

They were escorted by both British and American destroyers, although America was not yet at war, during the crossing of the Atlantic to Halifax, Nova Scotia. They onward travelled on the USS Wakefield, with a stop at Trinidad, to Cape Town, arriving on 8th December 1941 the day after the Japanese attack on Pearl Harbour.

Figure 207 USS Wakefield (formerly SS Manhattan)

After a four day stay in Cape Town, they were rerouted to the Far East setting sail and arriving in Bombay 14 days later. Following arrival in Bombay, (now Mumbai), they travelled to Poonah, (now Pune, a former garrison town of the British Army), staying for two weeks, upon which they were redirected back to the USS Wakefield for onward travel to reinforce Singapore.

The USS Wakefield departed for Singapore on 19th January 1942 and arrived on 29th January to find the island under attack by the Japanese. After only two weeks in Singapore, they became prisoners of war.

Surrender of Singapore and transfer to Thailand

The Japanese had taken most of Malaya by early 1942 and were only 30 miles from Singapore. They cut off the water supply to the British Garrison and Singapore residents. Following loss of the water supply, Lieutenant General Arthur Percival, the Singapore commander, was forced to surrender to the Japanese on 15th February 1942. British servicemen were taken as Prisoners of War and were probably detained in Selarang Barracks in Singapore.

Figure 208 The British surrender to the Japanese on 15th February 1942

The British soldiers in Singapore, including the three Burbage men Dobson, Letts and Tite, all were transported to Thailand. The prisoners arrived at a station in Thailand called Ban Pong. Here they learned that they were to be forced to build a railway which would enable the Japanese to expand through Thailand across Burma and into India.

Figure 209 Ban Pong Station, Thailand

A railway from Thailand to Burma had been surveyed pre-war and it had proved too costly in both time and labour. An estimated 60,000 labourers would be needed for 5 years. The Japanese did not have 5 years to dominate the region but they did have 250,000 prisoners of war as 'free' labour.

When the prisoners arrived, the railway line terminated at Ban Pong. From there, they were marched to their designated work sections; 25 miles to Kanchanaburi or 67 miles to Nam Tok. Upon reaching their final destinations, they were housed in bamboo huts.

Figure 210 Prisoners housed in Bamboo Huts

We are taken to Singapore railway station where we are crowded into steel cattle wagons. On average about 35 men to each of these wagons; about 30 of these made up a train. So, around 1000 men, plus guards with machine guns at the ready, we were on the move to Thailand.
What we are taken there for was anyone's guess. It took about four days to get to our destination. A journey I will never forget.
Most of us now were suffering from dysentery, and with no toiletry facilities being available, most of us were experiencing a very hectic time.
A lot of stoppages occurred as regular trains took priority over our train. So, when we stopped in a siding, nine times out of ten it would be in full sun, and being steel trucks, you can imagine what the temperature is like.

Account by: Sidney John Stebbeds of 5th Battalion, The Suffolk Regiment.

Private Dobson, Corporal Letts and Private Tite

After only two weeks in Singapore, their only experience of war, Harry Dobson and Jeffery Tite were captured and made prisoners of war.

The two friends found themselves in horrendous conditions. Corporal Harold Letts, another Burbage man was also in Singapore at the time of surrender and met the same fate becoming a prisoner of the Japanese. These three soldiers were forced to labour, and were literally slaves, compelled to work on the infamous Thailand to Burma Railway. There was little food or sanitation, and disease was rife. Jeffery Tite died first, on the 22nd September 1943, he was 24. Harold Letts died on the 9th October 1943 aged 29. and finally Harry Dobson died 2 months later, on the 11th December, he was also 24.

Memorial to those who died

The graves of those who died during the construction and maintenance of the Burma-Thailand railway (except for the Americans, whose remains were repatriated) were transferred from camp burial grounds and isolated sites along the railway into three cemeteries at Chungkai and Kanchanaburi in Thailand and Thanbyuzayat in Burma. Kanchanaburi War Cemetery is only a short distance from the site of the former 'Kanburi', the prisoner of war base camp through which most of the prisoners passed on their way to other camps. The cemetery was created by the Army Graves Service who transferred to it all graves along the southern section of railway, from Bangkok to Nieke.

Figure 211 Plaque in remembrance of those who died during captivity in the Far East

Military Deaths In Burbage

In addition to the loss of men from the Parish of Burbage, the village sadly was the location of at least two plane crashes, both of which resulted in fatalities. These devastating incidents were part of war and would have been associated with little public acknowledgement at the time. It would be sixty years after the crash, and following extensive research by Greg Drozdz, that public recognition would take place for the first of these incidents. At the time of writing the details of the second crash are still being researched in the hope that a further memorial can be erected.

Wellington Bomber MF-116

Figure 212 Memorial Plaque to Wellington Bomber MF116

The RAF faced the continual need to train pilots and aircrew to meet the demands of the evolving conflict. The Allied push into Europe required skilled personnel to support ground offensives, execute bombing campaigns, and maintain air superiority. Losses in combat and the introduction of advanced aircraft necessitated continuous recruitment and training to sustain operational strength. Furthermore, with the war in the Pacific still raging, preparing aircrew for potential redeployment was critical. In this context the crew of Wellington Bomber MF-116 set off on a training flight from RAF Wing in Oxfordshire.

It was at 14:15 hrs, just after lunch time, on Sunday 14th January 1945 that crews were briefed for the training exercise that night. It was planned that the flight, for Flying Officer Chobaniuk, would take his crew over Northampton, towards Cromer and a flight over the North Sea before returning along the same route. It was intended that this would be the last training flight of the crew before they transferred to operational duties. It was expected the flight would take almost 5½ hours. After a further briefing at about 16:00 hrs, Chobaniuk and his crew reported for the flight at about 17:15 hrs and Chobaniuk signed the authorisation book. The aircraft they would be flying that evening was a Vickers Wellington Mark X bomber.

At 18:05 hrs January 1945 the flight took off from the Wing airfield, in the Vale of Aylesbury. The aircraft number was MF-116. The aircraft would have headed towards Northampton as part of their flight plans. In the briefing the crew were given that afternoon, the Duty Signals Officer at RAF Wing informed them that strict wireless silence was to be observed throughout the entire trip. He emphasised that only in the event of an emergency should this silence be broken.

Little information is known about the flight out over the North Sea, partly due to the wireless silence and partly that the navigator's log was never recovered. However, at 10:15 hrs just over four hours into the flight some form of incident occurred on board. At this time it was anticipated the flight would be over Kingston-Upon-Hull. This has been deduced from details of the wireless operator's log which had been maintained up to this time but ended abruptly. It was assumed something happened which prevented the operator from continuing with his log.

It was not until 23:38 hrs that the Duty Control Officers at both RAF Bramcote and RAF Nuneaton heard a Mayday call from the aircraft. The emergency radio communication system used by the RAF during WW2 was known as the Darky Call system. It was designed as a backup navigation and communication aid for Allied aircraft, especially for those in distress or struggling to locate their home airfield, particularly during poor weather, at night, or when other navigation systems were unavailable. The Officer at RAF Nuneaton heard "Hullo Darky, Hello Darky, Hullow Darky, Mayday, Mayday, Mayday, from Furdle Dog". He immediately replied "Hullow Furdle Dog, Hullo Furdle Dog, what assistance do you require, what assistance do you require?". The officer at RAF Bramcote was unable to provide assistance as no night flying facilities were available; however, RAF Nuneaton immediately switched on landing lights at their station. No further contact was established between the aircraft and RAF Nuneaton or RAF Bramcote.

103

Three separate witnesses in Burbage estimated hearing an aircraft flying over the village at about 23:40 hrs with engines not performing in a normal manner, followed by the sound of a crash and then a sudden silence.

It was not until 08:50 hrs the next morning, Monday 15th January that the police in Hinckley received a report that wreckage of a plane had been found in Burbage, in a field at Holt Farm. In 1945 this area of Burbage was still open farmland with a stream known as Holt Burn flowing down towards Sketchley Brook near the boundary with Hinckley. Police Inspector John Edward Freestone immediately travelled to the site by car. Here Freestone found the wreckage spread over the width of a 3 acre field. It was found that all of the crew had died in the crash. At the investigation held at Bramcote the next day a Medical Orderly, based at Bramcote, reported he had been sent to the crash site. On arrival all of the crew had been recovered onto stretchers, he quickly inspected all of the crew and confirmed they were dead. All but one of the crew had severe head and body injuries and in his opinion the injuries of all of the crew were such that it is most likely they were killed instantly. He returned all of the bodies to RAF Bramcote where he was able to identify all of the crew, as they each had their identity discs.

The crew were:

- Flying Officer Nicholas Chobaniuk, R.C.A.F.
- Sergeant Leslie George Good, R.A.F.
- Sergeant John Sidney Gunn, R.A.F.
- Sergeant John William McMurdo, R.C.A.F.
- Sergeant Charles Dennis Parker, R.A.F.
- Sergeant John Thompson, R.A.F.

There was no newspaper report of the crash until one month later, when the investigation concluded, "The primary cause of the accident is considered to be the failure of the PORT engine, the cause of the engine failure being unknown. There is insufficient evidence to establish whether any error on the part of the pilot was a contributory cause of the accident". The aircraft was still travelling at a considerable speed when the port wing tip hit the ground with only the Starboard engine working at the time of impact. There was speculation that the pilot may have mistook street lights of Hinckley as a flarepath.

The story of the aircraft crash in Burbage quickly disappeared from news and it is likely no further thought would have been given to the event. However, in 2004 local historian Greg Drozdz researched the story and discovered the investigation papers. He prompted the Burbage Parish Council to recognise the loss of these six airman in the village. The Council immediately took up this challenge and arranged for a memorial for the airman at the site of the crash.

NOBODY HEARD BOMBER CRASH NEAR HINCKLEY

A REMARKABLE story lies behind the crashing of a Wellington bomber in fields between Hinckley and Burbage on the night of January 14. About midnight, when most people had gone to bed, a sound, obviously from a plane in difficulties, was heard overhead. People who were still downstairs rushed from their home, but nothing could be seen and nothing was heard of an actual crash.

Many people, believing that the plane had righted itself and proceeded on its way went indoors again. Others formed themselves into search parties, but could find no trace of a crash.

A farmworker named Raven, living at Sketchley, heard a bump, but neither heard nor saw anything else, and he, too, came to the conclusion that nothing untoward had happened.

The following morning he went out into the fields and found the wrecked plane, which had crashed 200 yards from his home. The bodies of the six RAF men were recovered.

In its swoop to earth the plane, which, it is thought, had run short of petrol, narrowly missed the houses on the Sketchley-road side of Hinckley.

The absence of any explosion, or even a light, handicapped would-be rescuers in finding the spot. Had the earlier search been successful, there is a possibility that some of the crew would have been saved.

Left: Figure 213
Leicester Evening Mail 16th February 1945

By this time the site was in the residential area of Featherston Drive. A decision was taken by the Parish Council to hold a Service of Dedication with representation from the RAF, Canadian Embassy, Royal British Legion and Local Air cadets.

By the time of the dedication ceremony on 14th January 2005, exactly sixty years after the fatal crash, members of some of the British victims had been found and they were overwhelmed that a memorial had been created. Many did not know the details of the final flight of their family member. Following the installation of the memorial Greg Drozdz was able to contact some of the Canadian family members who were equally grateful that this new memorial had been created.

The ceremony was opened by Parish Chairman Cllr Don Bayley and prayers were led by the Rector Fr David Jennings. At the services held in 2005 and 2025 Greg Drozdz spoke of the story and ended by reading the poem For Johnny by John Pudney.

For Johnny

Do not despair
For Johnny-head-in-air;
He sleeps as sound
As Johnny underground.

Fetch out no shroud
For Johnny-in-the-cloud;
And keep your tears
For him in after years.

Better by far
For Johnny-the-bright-star,
To keep your head,
And see his children fed.

John Sleigh Pudney

During World War II, John Pudney was commissioned into the Royal Air Force as an intelligence officer and as a member of the Air Ministry's Creative Writers Unit.

Figure 214 Famous poem by John Pudney

Six Killed When Bomber Crashed Near Hinckley

A remarkable story lies behind the crashing of a Wellington bomber in fields between Hinckley and Burbage on the night of Jan. 14th.

It was about midnight, and most folk had retired to their beds when suddenly a "swooping" sound, obviously from a 'plane in difficulties, was heard overhead. People who were still downstairs rushed from their homes to ascertain the cause, but nothing could be seen and nothing was heard of an actual crash. Many people, believing that the 'plane had righted itself and proceeded on its way, went indoors again. Others formed themselves into search parties but could find no trace of a crash.

A farm worker named Raven, living at Sketchley, heard a distinct bump, but neither heard nor saw anything else, and he, too, came to the conclusion that nothing untoward had happened.

The following morning he went out into the fields and found the wrecked 'plane, which had crashed 200 yards from his home. The bodies of the six R.A.F. men were recovered.

NARROWLY MISSED SKETCHLEY ROAD HOUSES

In its swoop to earth the 'plane, which it is thought had run short of petrol, narrowly missed the houses on the Sketchley Road side of Hinckley.

The absence of any explosion or even a light handicapped would-be rescuers in finding the spot. Had the earlier search been more successful there is a likelihood that some of the crew might have been saved.

The pilot was a Canadian and the aircraft had come from a Buckinghamshire station.

Figure 215 Hinckley Times and Guardian 16th February 1945

Figure 216 Bomber Memorial 80th Anniversary 2025

Flying Officer Nicholas Chobaniuk

Royal Canadian Air Force died on 14th January 1945 Age 25
Service Number: J/23790

Nicholas was the son of Paul and Nettie Chobaniuk. He was born and raised in Regina, Saskatchewan, Canada. His parents were Romanian and had become Canadian citizens. He had six living brothers, the eldest of these was Michael who was also in the Royal Canadian Air Force, based in England. Sadly on the night Nicholas was killed Michael was on leave and had been staying at RAF Wing with his brother and therefore would have been extremely anxious when Nicholas' flight did not return.

In a letter home to Mrs Chobaniuk, his Commanding Officer notified her that Nicholas' funeral would take place in Chester on Friday 19th January and that three Canadian Officers and three Canadian N.C.O.s from the station would attend and wreaths would be sent. He also told her that he had made arrangements for his brother Michael to attend the funeral. He told her that Nicholas had been under his command for three months, during which time all had formed a very high opinion of him.

> Remembered with Honour
> CHESTER (BLACON) CEMETERY
> Sec. A. Grave 844.

Sergeant Leslie George Good

Royal Air Force Volunteer Reserve died on 14th January 1945 Age 20
Service Number: 1808623

Leslie was the only child of Edward George and Lilian Good, of Forest Gate, London. He was buried 800 yards from where his parents lived, in Manor Park Cemetery, London

> HE GAVE HIS YOUNG LIFE FOR FREEDOM.
> GOD GRANT HIM ETERNAL REST
> Remembered with Honour
> MANOR PARK CEMETERY
> Sec. 54. Grave 503.

Sergeant John Sidney Gunn

Royal Air Force Volunteer Reserve died on 14th January 1945 Age 22
Service Number: 1804820

John was the son of Edwin John Charles and Edith Fanny Gunn, of North Harrow, Middlesex. John's Mother died soon after the birth of his younger sister when John was about one year old

> UNTIL THE DAY BREAK AND
> THE SHADOWS FLEE AWAY
> Remembered with Honour
> OXFORD (BOTLEY) CEMETERY
> Plot H/1. Grave 242.

Sergeant John William McMurdo

Royal Canadian Air Force died on 14th January 1945 Age 33
Service Number: R/67119

John was the son of John and Amy McMurdo of Ontario, Canada. His father was from Scotland and his mother from Yorkshire. John, Known as 'Jack' married Elva Agnes Sharpe in October 1932. They had three daughters between 1933 and 1935 and they lived in Cobourg, Ontario, Canada. Jack was buried in Chester, England.

> IN LIFE, LOVED AND HONOURED IN DEATH,
> EVER REMEMBERED
> Remembered with Honour
> CHESTER (BLACON) CEMETERY
> Sec. A. Grave 1025.

Sergeant Charles Dennis Parker

Royal Air Force Volunteer Reserve died on 14th January 1945 Age 19
Service Number: 3041583

Charles was the son of Percy and Edith Parker, of Kiveton Park, West Riding of Yorkshire.

> WORTHY OF EVERLASTING REMEMBRANCE.
> SERVER AND CHORISTER OF THIS CHURCH
> Remembered with Honour
> WALES (ST. JOHN THE BAPTIST) CHURCHYARD

Sergeant John Thompson

Royal Air Force Volunteer Reserve died on 14th January 1945 Age 23
Service Number: 1059098

John was the son of Robert and Elizabeth Thompson of Carlisle.

> Remembered with Honour
> CARLISLE (DALSTON ROAD) CEMETERY
> Ward 16. Sec. O. Grave 101.

Figure 217 Relatives of the fallen lay wreaths in 2005

Figure 218 Photograph of six memorial bushes at the site of the crash, each having a named brass plaque.

Wellington Bomber X9953

On January 9th 1943, a Vickers Wellington Mk 1c X9953, part of 18 Operational Training Unit (OTU), took off from RAF Westcott on the Oxfordshire/Buckinghamshire border, her two Bristol Pegasus Radial engines hauling her and her crew of 5 up into the growing dark.

They had no bomb load, as this was just a simple night-time cross country navigational training flight. As the crew settled down for the flight, little did they know how it would end.

The five crew consisted of trainees and mixed nationalities, all drawn together for one cause.

- Cyril Hoy (Pilot) RAF
- V.J. Sharp RNZAF
- J.E. Hoey RAF
- I. Tvrdeich RNZAF
- E.J. Mansell RAF

The crew had a mixture of skills; navigation, wireless and air gunners.

The weather that night was cold and wet, with recent snowfall and only 13% moon visible. Just before midnight things started to go wrong. It would seem that the pilot was flying in cloud, against instructions, (but he may have had little option due to the weather) when the Wellington started to become difficult to handle, increasingly so as the aeroplane started to ice up. Icing is an extremely dangerous thing; it changes the aeroplane's aerodynamics to that of a paving slab. They were losing height fast, despite efforts by the pilot to remedy the situation. He ordered the crew to abandon the aircraft.

They bailed out at a very low height of just 800 ft, hardly any time for their parachutes to deploy properly.

Very shortly after X9953 ran out of sky. The aircraft hit the ground near or on Mickle Hill, south east of Lutterworth Road Burbage, around 01.00 hrs and burst into flames on impact.

Sadly, the pilot did not survive the crash. At present whether he jumped or remained with the aircraft isn't clear. All members of the crew except for the pilot survived the crash. These casualties were taken to Orchard farm. The pilot's remains were recovered.

The rest of his crew after treatment were returned to their base, and after further training, were posted to Heavy Bomber Squadrons. Unfortunately, only Pilot Officer E.J. Mansell, of the crew that night, would go on to survive the war.

Michael Wyles of Burbage recalls "I first heard about the incident when I was a small child. I was told by an old village character, Harry Judkins, how he had witnessed what he described 'the bodies' being taken in to Orchard farm."

Michael has been researching further details of the crash and recovery operation and hopes to discover enough about the event such that a memorial can be placed to record this sad accident.

Michael reflects "How many brave young men lost their lives during courageous raids over enemy territory, going and returning. These are rightly commemorated and remembered, however many others, like poor Cyril, pushed through their training, never had the chance and their sacrifice, for it was so, as much as any operational crews, remains largely unmentioned."

The crash raises several questions that remain unanswered: Did Cyril stay at the controls to ensure his crew's safety or attempt to land on open ground, considering Burbage, Aston, and Sharnford were nearby? Did the wireless operator send a May Day signal? Was the Navigator accurately plotting the route? Did any local aerodromes receive any signals, and why were they unable to reach one of them safely despite their proximity?

Cyril Hoy RAF

RAF Volunteer Reserve died on 10th January 1943 Age 25
Service Number: 1316783

Cyril was the son of Herbert and Agnes Dorothea Hoy, of Hull.

> AT THE GOING DOWN OF THE SUN AND IN THE MORNING WE WILL REMEMBER THEM
> Remembered with Honour
> HULL EASTERN CEMETERY
> Compt. 158. Joint grave 27.

Cyril was trained in Canada, as were many RAF pilots, his rank Sergeant. With a total of 213 flying hours under his belt, but only 40 at night, 58 hours on Wellingtons with just 25 of these night flying!

After the crash Cyril's remains were recovered and buried in his hometown of Hull. Sadly, for the family the tragedy would not end here, only four weeks later his brother Stanley was killed on a Lancaster bomber training flight on the 12th February 1943. Mr & Mrs Hoy gave two of their three sons to the cause of freedom.

Yanks For The Memory

"…..Coming to Hinckley and Burbage after being under fire for 60 days at Anzio was like going to Heaven and not having to die to get there…."

Captain Paul Donnelly

So, what was heaven like?

The 307th Airborne Engineers of the American 82nd Airborne Division arrived in Burbage on 12th February 1944. They were to be joined by the 376th Parachute Field Artillery who arrived in Hinckley a little later on 23rd April 1944.

They were battle hardened veterans in need of rest and recuperation and Burbage would provide this in spades. Over a short period of months the unit made themselves at home and were welcomed by most, although their access to supplies and rations caused envy amongst some. War was never far from their experience as they prepared to be involved in D Day in June and Operation Market Garden in September.

Pubs, the movies, dances, an Anglo-American Welcome Club, churches and chapels, it must have seemed a little like home. For their part the Americans would bring extra rations, powdered egg, Hershey bars, chewing gum, the jitterbug, nylons, increased income for local retail businesses and Baseball. Although they may have been two nations divided by a common language, the Americans were quickly befriended by British families and by the children of the village especially.

Initially housing a large number of GIs must have been a difficult logistical exercise but the empty Moore, Eady, Murcott Goode factory in the centre of the village, provided space for the majority of the troops. The building was then forever known as the Barracks. The overflow was housed in tents where the Millenium Hall now stands behind the factory. Eventually a company of the unit would be based out at Ullesthorpe. Officers' quarters were situated elsewhere – at Burbage Hall at one end of the village and at the Hinckley Knight hotel at the Three Pots end of the village.

From the American point of view, Staff Sergeant Frank Miale recorded his impressions of the village in a little detail in his book *"Stragedy"*. Sylvia Whitworth of the Burbage Heritage group collected a series of impressions of the time from local people who lived through the heady days of the summer of 1944.

Figure 219 The interior of Burbage Hall

Miale commented on one particular incident. He recalled three colleagues, Perkins, Finney and Hughes purchasing crates of pale ale to then consume at their own leisure. The imbibing took place off military premises in a field next to where a flock of sheep were grazing watched over by English sheepdogs. One of the dogs, curious at the aroma of the ale approached the three GIs and was encouraged by them to imbibe as well. The dog followed them back to barracks and slept off a hangover under Perkins' cot. The owner, unhappy that the dog was not working told the GIs that they could keep the dog and that is how *"Corned Beef"* became the company mascot. "He got to know everyone in the company and wouldn't let any strangers come into the compound unless they were with someone he knew. He loved the adulation afforded him by the men and he seemed to strut as he led many a parade or hike in which the company participated."

"THERE'LL ALWAYS BE AN ENGLAND"

—WHILE THERE'S A HINCKLEY!

—"Spike," of the Yanks

A popular member of the American Forces stationed at Hinckley some twelve months ago was Sergeant "Spike" Lynch, who made the acquaintance of many people in this locality. He has since been badly wounded in the fighting on the Western Front and is now back in America where he has undergone several operations.

Writing to Mr. and Mrs. Les. Simpson, of "Greenacres" Sketchley, Hinckley, "Spike" says: "I miss you folk something awful. I feel a vacant space in my heart, and not having Dannie, George and the boys, makes it worst. As I lie here in my bed awaiting further operations I think of you folk many times and of the fun we had together, and of those nights we had in the smoking rooms at Hinckley—the fun that was caused when the towels were up. I was never so homesick for England, Hinckley and Burbage as I am now. Imagine that coming from an Irishman pining for ' my dear friends ' in England.

"You people were grand to me. Some day I'll come back and return the favour. When I went home my sisters could not understand my attitude. The folk in Hinckley have done more in creating friends with those in America than all the big diplomats in the British Empire and in America.

WILL ALWAYS REMEMBER HINCKLEY

"My only wish is that the boys will be able to come back to see you. In their letters they always mention Hinckley. Please God I'll be able to come back just as soon as the war is over, and from all accounts it won't be long. Every time I think of all those fine chaps I met at Hinckley it hurts to know that I had to leave it all behind. To forget Hinckley is something that will never happen. The people there will always be in my mind and I shall miss you very much. Please say ' Hello ' to all those dear friends in Hinckley and extend my very best for their kindness to me in the past. To express my deep gratitude is one thing I can faithfully do. There'll always be an England while there are such fine people as I met in Hinckley. God bless you all and may the future be bright and merry."

Mr. Simpson has addressed a suitable reply reciprocating the kind wishes and expressing the hope that the American boys will again be permitted to spent a further vacation in Hinckley.

BURBAGE FALLEN OF THE SECOND WORLD WAR

Of the villagers, Pat Chapman recalled: *"I remember going up to the Barracks with my sister and seeing the Yanks standing around outside, along with the other kids in the village they would give us gum and chocolate. My Mum was in the Red Lion one night when an American came in and asked if anyone would do the washing and ironing. Dad was not very pleased about Mum doing this, but she was glad of the extra money. As a nine-year-old I remember thinking how handsome and smart they were when they came to collect the washing."* Mavis White recalled that: *"People were encouraged to invite troops around for baths and meals. Two American officers I recall were Cyr (Euclid Cyr) and Wally (Ed Whalen)".* In many homes baths must have been tin baths in front of the fire. The bathing facilities at the Barracks were severely limited.

The Anglo-American club, established at the Working Men's Club in Hinckley, was an attempt to provide an environment away from the pubs and the movies, at the three cinemas in the town. Clare Smith of Burbage recalled: *"I offered to do voluntary work helping in a canteen at the working men's club in Holliers Walk. We made sandwiches, cakes and served tea and other refreshments and opened three or four evenings a week. Living in Coventry Road, Burbage meant a walk home after work as the last bus left at 7pm (Robinsons 3d return to Hinckley)".* There was a similar set up established at the Wesleyan School rooms in Burbage.

A number of families agreed to write to the families back in the USA on behalf of the GIs. Military letters were subject to censorship but not so civilian letters. In this way families across the Atlantic came to know each other. Those friendships abide to this day. A natural consequence of the mingling of the nationalities were not only platonic relationships but relationships for life. There were a number of GI brides from the village – marrying men such as Ted Visneski, Vernon Watters, Florian Couture, Travis Womack, Ralph Clausen and Frank Miale.

THANKS TO THE PEOPLE OF BURBAGE

Sir,—I write this letter to fulfil a promise made to the soldiers who were stationed in Burbage during the war. Before leaving the village most of them asked me to express on their behalf thanks and gratitude to all who offered them the use of baths and homes. They asked that this expression of thanks should be made when the war was over.

U. HINCKS.

Coventry Road,
Burbage.

Figure 220 Hinckley Times 31st August 1945

Left: Figure 221 Hinckley Times 20th April 1945

Figure 222 Florian Couture and Betty Campton

There was also the concomitant difficulty of pregnancies outside of marriage for some of the local women. The resulting births were often shrouded in mystery for a number of years, as the serviceman involved was moved on, never to return. However, there are local people who have contacted their birth fathers, years later, to find that they have been welcomed with open arms. This phenomenon was known at the time as "slip". To counter it the American authorities set up brothels where the GIs could assuage their urges, with free condoms provided. There was one such establishment in Burbage.

The 82nd Airborne Division were known as the "All Americans", in that there were men enlisted from every state in the USA. There were whites, Hispanics and Chinese Americans but no Black Americans. Segregation at home meant segregation in the army. There were separate Black American units. However, a few people in Burbage remembered a Black America. Kathleen Robbins said: "*A black American was so surprised when he came to Burbage because people were so nice to him and he was well treated by the locals…. one local girl married a Black American but the village midwife was not aware of this, so when the baby was born, imagine her surprise*". John Newton recalled how naive he had been: "*Soon after their arrival I saw my first black man. I innocently asked if the black rubbed off and he laughed his head off showing all his white teeth*".

Speaking with the late Arthur Cross, he said that there had been a Black American in Burbage, driving a jeep or a lorry to collect stores from Leicester. He always came back with "*contraband*", items like whisky etc, which created a vibrant black market amongst the troops and likely involving some of the residents, as well.

Figure 223 A Black American soldier with friends in Hinckley

Figure 224 Baseball on the Burbage, Hinckley Road, Recreation ground

Another villager, Derek Farnell recorded that his mother and aunty would go to dances organised by the Yanks, especially as they knew there would be a good buffet. Dances in Burbage took place in the Co-op Hall and concerts took place in the upstairs of the Wesleyan School in Windsor Street. The GIs did attend local church services. Frank Miale organised a fund-raising effort amongst his fellow Catholics to have altar rails installed in St Peter's Church in Hinckley, at the top of Wood Street.

The expanse of the recreation ground off Hinckley Road, at the rear of Forresters Road, proved too much of an allure and baseball matches were arranged, where the intricacies of the game were explained and practiced before large crowds. John Newton said: "*We loved watching them play baseball as it was a new game to us. During one baseball match I was hit in the leg and they were so sorry they carried me home and showered me with chocolates and comics*". Home run!

The one area where advantage was taken of the Americans was money! "The troops always had plenty of money and many had no concept of what a pound was worth. They would give us a £5 note for buckets of beer, when beer was 3d a pint" recalled John Newton. To a child's enquiry of: "*Got any gum chum?*", the GI reply was: "*sure thing kid. Say you got a pretty sister?*" John also said: "We kids had a whale of a time with the Yanks and they brightened up our lives immensely and left us with many happy memories".

There was a serious side to the Americans stay in the area. They did practice jumps in preparation for their next operation, which for the 307th was to be involved with the parachute landings around St Mere Eglise. Some of those leaving the village in the days before the invasion would not return.

GIs FROM BURBAGE KILLED IN NORMANDY

Foon G Chin	Karl J Leverknight
John I Connelley Jr	Benjamin I McKeeby
Ralph J Cunningham	Daniel J O'Neill
Moses de Souza	John J O'Neill
James I Durham	Elmer Q Siddall
Charlie K Edmondson Jr	Alexander F Sweeney
Elmer Ellis	Paul D Wheeler
Horace Joseph	Preston S Wright
Ropy K Kreiser	William W Yeo
Everette H Langford	Paul W Yonkin

Frank Miale, who survived the Normandy campaign, felt some bitterness when he returned as promotions seemed to be being given to the replacements who were joining the unit and not to those who had participated in the brutal battles for French villages and hedgerows. Vernon Watters returned, having been missing in action for 14 days and living on rations until he could find and return to his unit in the field.

It would not be long before orders were issued for the second planned invasion of 1944, Operation Market Garden, the attempt to spring into Holland and then proceed towards Berlin. Both the Engineers from Burbage and the Artillery from Hinckley would be involved this time. The artillery unit in Hinckley had not participated in Normandy.

Villagers would recall that this time, the Americans were gone for good with only a cadre base camp left behind to clear up the men's possessions and the detritus left behind, as the war moved permanently onto the continent of Europe. Sadly, again some of those previously billeted in Burbage would lose their lives in Holland.

GIs FROM BURBAGE KILLED IN HOLLAND

John M Baer	James A Jacobs
Charles M Billeter	Willard Jenkins
Kenneth R Carlson	Willam E Kero
Alfred H Conrad	Stanley W King
Stanley J Czuhajewski	Emerson A Lum
Fred H Durben	William W Martin
Earl E Easterbrook	Robert I Mottern
Lawrence I Fainelli	James Murray
William W Felgenhauer	Robert S Opacich
Harry G Fowler	Ralph C Pulliam
Herman R Fuller	George C Rudin
Louis F Gentile	James S Stephenson
Willam B Harris	Carl C Tole
Robert Hause	Herbert R Wendland
Edward V Henschler	James F Woods
Herman I Jacobius	

The Americans may have suddenly gone but friendships endured. Veterans did, occasionally, return to the village on visits, although as their ranks diminished, so it became the sons and daughters and their families who travelled back. In 2004, both Frank Miale and Vernon Watters were in Burbage. Vern and his GI bride, Betty, came to hear a talk given at the Millennium Hall by myself, entitled *"Yanks for the Memory"*. This complemented an exhibition at the Hinckley and District Museum, with the same title. Frank and his GI bride, Sadie, were guests of honour at the Sycamores Pub to unveil a plaque commemorating the American stay in Burbage. There was a fly past over the village by a C-47 Dakota in invasion stripes and there were re-enactors on the ground. Recently, a further plaque was inaugurated in Hinckley, providing American visitors with a meeting and discussion point. As the plaque (see photo on page 132) on the Sycamores says:

"may the bonds of kinship and friendship forged in the crucible of war endure forever".

POLES APART

Figure 225 H M King George VI taking the salute of the Polish servicemen at RAF Bramcote 20th August 1940

In the early years of the Second World War there was locally in Burbage and Hinckley a large influx of Polish servicemen associated with RAF Bramcote, just the other side of the Watling Street from Burbage.

It was early in 1939 that construction began on the airfield, and it was built to the highest of specifications, with attractive brick buildings, spacious accommodation and tarmacadamed roads and good working conditions. Yet when the first English crews arrived it was still not finished. From November 1939, 18 OTU (18 Operational Training Unit) arrived, and this was special – it was a Polish training unit with its associated ground crew.

The Poles had been the first to fight...their country had been invaded by the Nazis and Russia in September of 1939. Many of the airmen, including Henry Drozdz, made their way via third countries, such as Romania and a Mediterranean boat journey, to France and formed squadrons at Bron-Lyon – the so-called Free Poles. Meanwhile in November 1939, the Polish authorities in exile, namely General Wladyslaw Sikorski, formed the basis of an agreement with the British to take 2,300 Polish airmen to form Polish Squadrons under RAF control, via a clearing station at RAF Eastchurch in Kent. The airmen would have to learn operational English and the new Squadrons would have a shared officer cadre between the Poles and the British.

With the airfield construction completed, the first Polish Squadron - a bomber squadron – 300 (Masovian) Polish Squadron was formed on 1st July 1940 and the local link with the Poles became deep rooted. The Poles were seen as VIPs, especially for propaganda purposes. Here was a country *"plighting its troth"* to the Allied cause. Churchill always had one eye on persuading the Americans to join the war, and the co-operation of the Poles gave him an opportunity to show solidarity.

On 3rd August Air Chief Marshall Sir Charles Portal, head of Bomber Command, visited to inspect the facilities and the airmen. On 20th August, HM King George VI visited, via Nuneaton railway station. Initially the Poles flew Fairey Battles but later converted to Wellington aircraft. The Poles availed themselves of the local fleshpots including, Nuneaton, Hinckley and Burbage.

The new Squadrons emerging from Bramcote had English officers attached to them. Adjutant of 18 OTU was Squadron Leader Sidney Kellaway, (see page 60) who lived off base in Brockhurst Avenue, Burbage. In conversation with Greg Drozdz, the late Eric Kellaway, the son of Sidney, recalled an incident that happened in 1941, which is captured on the next page.

Greg Drozdz also gives a family reflection of Polish aircrew's arrival at Bramcote.

Eric Kellaway recalling a local Wellington Bomber Crash

The telephone rang. It was the base alerting my father to a crash on the Wolvey Road, of a Polish aircraft, a Wellington bomber. He grabbed me, got into his car and dashed off in the direction of Wolvey to see if we could find out what had happened. We were just past Leicester Grange, before what is now Asfare Business Park, when we saw flames off to the left in the trees. We got out and ran to the scene. It was a nightmare.

Figure 226 The effects of fire on the frame of a Wellington bomber.

We could see the crashed fuselage, all on fire. The canvas was literally being peeled from the geodetic frame by the flames. We could see the Poles inside, attempting furiously and unsuccessfully to find a way out. They were screaming at the top of their heads. The screams were piercing, I will never forget them. Slowly, they got less and less as the young Poles succumbed to the flames and the fire. There was a dreadful smell of burning engine oil and petrol. The air was acrid with smoke. I could not believe what I had seen. A later Court of Enquiry demanded that all such aircraft be fitted with axes which could be used to hack at the air frame to effect and escape from any burning aircraft. The remains of the bodies were buried in Nuneaton.

A Family Reflection of the RAF Bramcote Legacy

There will be young Polish families currently in Hinckley and Burbage who may not even know that their language, heard every day in the town and village, was being spoken 80 years ago in the very same places. For those Poles working at nearby Magna Park, this is particularly poignant as that was the site of a Polish airfield- RAF Bitteswell, initially a grass airfield.

In 1941, RAF Bitteswell was opened as an airfield, affiliated to RAF Bramcote. The conditions there were far from congenial. My Father recalled in a wartime diary that he kept that he was billeted in a tent, sleeping on the ground. He considered this as a nadir of his time so far, recalling ironically his scouting days in the woods around Warsaw.

The Poles at Bramcote were encouraged, particularly through the local Catholic churches, to befriend local families. Lifelong friendships were fostered in this way. Several of the Poles married local girls, including my father. In 1943 18 OTU moved to Finningley in Yorkshire, but the bonds of friendship and kinship were now truly so embedded as to endure.

After the cessation of hostilities in May 1945, the lines of the new Europe had already been drawn and Poland was consigned to the Soviet bloc. That the Poles felt thus betrayed is an understatement. Adding ignominy to ignominy they were not allowed to take part in the 1946 Victory parade through London, to appease the Soviets.

The question of demobilisation was contentious, as the trade unions felt that Poles staying in the country would take up jobs of British workers and put a strain on other facilities.

Figure 227 Two of the Bramcote Poles, my father (Henryk Drozdz) on the right, the one with the distinctive "Poland" shoulder flash.

Consequently, Canada and Australia were persuaded to accept large numbers of Poles. Post war, some Poles were allowed to stay and became naturalised British citizens. Polish refugees in Europe came to this country. It is not surprising then that in Burbage and Hinckley that a few Poles would settle after the war. At least two Poles lived in Burbage, Cechlacz and Rygielski and three or four in Hinckley – Pakula, Mostowy, Drozdz and Szmidt. It was the major manufacturing areas of Leicester and Nottingham though that attracted greater numbers of the settlers.

The heavy accented Poles found a way to survive in this brave new world. They settled in, passively, to an English way of life with their English families. All was not harmonious though. One Pole, being refused a "mate's rate" at the Polish jeweller, Mostowy, at the top of the Lawns Hinckley was disgusted that the previous shared war experience seemed now to have turned on its head. The Free Poles of the war years found it difficult to relate to those post war refugees. After all, they had fought for the right to be in the country. My Father shared a work bench at Burgess Products with a refugee Pole, Szmidt. He would not converse directly with him only through third party onlookers.

Some of the settling Poles changed their names by deed poll to English surnames, to avoid awkward exchanges. At least one of these lived in Burbage, I believe, with the surname of Woodward. Michal Barewski became Michael Burdett of Nuneaton.

RAF Bramcote is still Ministry of Defence property, but the outlines of the old airfield can still be made out, with the now isolated concrete pill boxes that still survive on the old perimeter of the airfield.

GREG DROZDZ

Churches, Chapels And Other Memorials

St Catherine's Parish Church

A parish church has existed in Burbage since the 12th Century and is dedicated to St Catherine of Alexandria. This Church together with the 11th Century Church of St Peter at Aston Flamville today form the Parish of Burbage and Aston Flamville. The present church at Burbage was rebuilt in 1842 - 1845 with the recent addition of a refectory to the north of the church in 2010.

At the outbreak of World War One, the Patronage of St Catherine's church was held by Auberon Thomas Herbert (1876-1916), Baron Lucas, who was also the Lord of the Manor of Burbage. At the outbreak of War, Lord Lucas was in the Asquith cabinet, holding the position of President of the Board of Agriculture and Fisheries. He left the government following the formation of the coalition government, in May 1915. Lord Lucas later served as a captain in the Royal Flying Corps in the First World War.

Auberon's sister, Nan Ino Herbert ran the family estate, Wrest Park, on her brother's behalf, although neither sibling used the house as a family home. Before war broke out, she had trained as a nurse and then went on to take over setting up and running Wrest Park, as a hospital for wounded soldiers until a fire at the house forced its early closure.

Whilst flying over German lines in November 1916, Lord Lucas' aircraft was attacked and brought down by a German fighter-aeroplane, and Auberon died of wounds whilst a prisoner of war the same day. Following the death of her brother, Nan Hebert inherited the Barony of Lucas becoming Lady Lucas.

Lady Lucas passed the patronage of St Catherine's to Balliol College, Oxford, in memory of her brother, Auberon, who had studied at the college.

Inside St Catherine's a carved wooden memorial was commissioned listing the names of 60 village men who died in WW1. Following WW2 a new additional carved memorial was commissioned listing the names of 31 village men who died in the war.

Figure 228 St Catherine's Church, Burbage

Figure 229 St Catherine's WW2 Memorial

Figure 230 St Catherine's Church - Plaque to the memory of Frederick Howarth

Figure 231 St Catherine's Church - Plaque to the memory of John Lord

In additional to the carved memorial above, individual plaques were installed in the church to recognise the roles Frederick Howarth and John Lord played in the service of St Catherines church.

Wesleyan Chapel

At the time of the First World War the Wesleyan Chapel was about 54 years old, the foundation stones being laid in 1860. The chapel was built upon the site of an earlier Chapel. The site also included a day school for the children of Burbage. This building was replaced in 2016 by a more contemporary flexible use design.

A plaque shown on the next page was installed on the altar rail of the chapel. When the chapel was remodelled in 1983 the memorial was saved from loss by Kate Chandler whose family now keep it safe. The names of H. Howkins, H. Letts, F Holyland and D. Wood are recorded on this plaque, see Figure 233.

Right: Figure 232 Wesleyan Chapel, Windsor Street, Burbage

Figure 233 Wesleyan Methodist Church, Burbage - Memorial to WW2 Fallen

Congregational Chapel

The Congregational Chapel stands on the corner of the Horsepool and Church Street. A smaller Chapel, built in 1860, was originally on the site. In 1895 this original chapel was demolished and the current larger chapel, replaced it. It was in the current Chapel, that several of the Burbage Fallen would have worshiped together with their families. Due to the stability of the front of the chapel, the chapel front was rebuilt early in the twentieth century, this rebuilding removed the large centre window and moved the two upper windows towards the centre of the building. The picture of the chapel today, no different to that at the time of WW2, is shown below.

In 1926 a new organ for the Chapel was commissioned and installed in 1927 as a WW1 memorial to the fallen of the Chapel. The plaque is still seen in the Chapel today.

A second plaque was erected after WW2 to record those who died in this war. The names of C.F. Barnes, S.C. Comer, D.S. Comer, H Dobson and J. Tite are recorded on this plaque.

Figure 234 Congregational Church, Burbage and Memorial to WW2 Fallen

St Peter's Roman Catholic Church, Hinckley

St Peter's Roman Catholic Church in Hinckley, Leicestershire, was originally built in 1824 and was a striking building renowned for its Gothic Revival architecture. The church featured intricate stonework, stunning stained-glass windows, and a welcoming atmosphere. However, it was demolished in the 1970s. A new church had been constructed in 1958 to accommodate the growing congregation, but due to structural faults, this church was also demolished in the early 1990s. The current St Peter's Church now stands on land to the east of the original site. The name of Burbage Fallen R.J. Kearns is recorded on the Memorial.

Right: Figure 235 St Peter's Roman Catholic Church, Hinckley War Memorial.

Right: Figure 236 St Peter's WW2 names.

Hinckley Grammar School

The Hinckley Grammar School memorial plaque to those pupils of the school who lost their lives in WW2 is now in the custody of Hinckley & District Museum. The memorial takes the form of a solid brass engraved metal plate which required six fixing holes due to its weight. The names of the Burbage fallen who are recorded on this memorial are; K.B. Lockton, J. Lord, S.R. Lount and T.F. Smith.

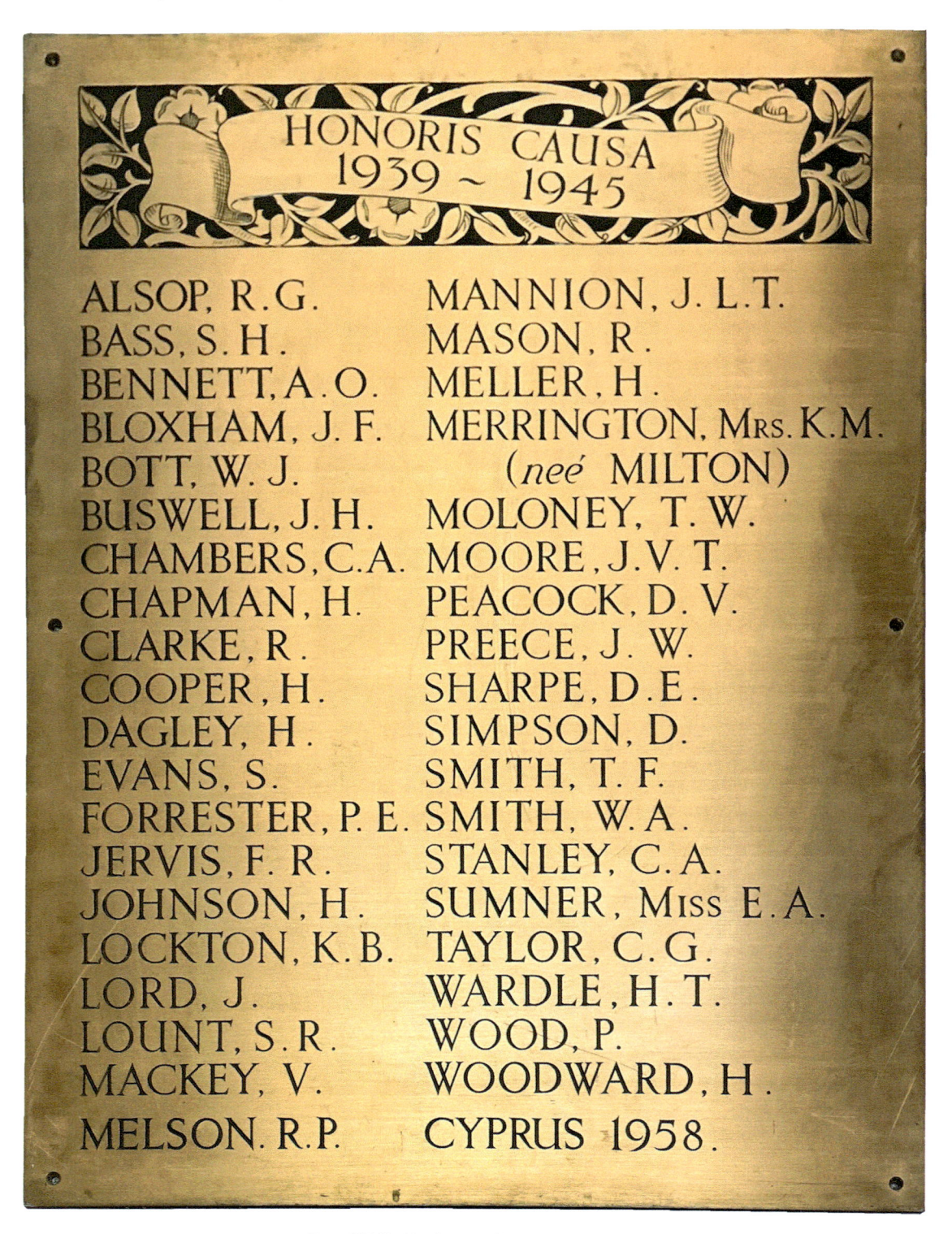

HONORIS CAUSA 1939 ~ 1945

ALSOP, R.G.
BASS, S.H.
BENNETT, A.O.
BLOXHAM, J.F.
BOTT, W.J.
BUSWELL, J.H.
CHAMBERS, C.A.
CHAPMAN, H.
CLARKE, R.
COOPER, H.
DAGLEY, H.
EVANS, S.
FORRESTER, P.E.
JERVIS, F.R.
JOHNSON, H.
LOCKTON, K.B.
LORD, J.
LOUNT, S.R.
MACKEY, V.
MELSON, R.P.

MANNION, J.L.T.
MASON, R.
MELLER, H.
MERRINGTON, Mrs. K.M. (neé MILTON)
MOLONEY, T.W.
MOORE, J.V.T.
PEACOCK, D.V.
PREECE, J.W.
SHARPE, D.E.
SIMPSON, D.
SMITH, T.F.
SMITH, W.A.
STANLEY, C.A.
SUMNER, Miss E.A.
TAYLOR, C.G.
WARDLE, H.T.
WOOD, P.
WOODWARD, H.
CYPRUS 1958.

Figure 237 Hinckley Grammar School Memorial Plaque.

Burbage Liberal Club

The Burbage Liberal Club, situated on Lutterworth Road in Burbage, Leicestershire, was established over a century ago as a prominent social and political hub. It provided a meeting place for the local community to discuss ideas and host events, fostering a sense of community and engagement. The club also served as a venue for various recreational activities, offering a social space for residents to gather and connect.

Over the decades, the club became a well-known landmark in the area, adapting to the changing needs of the community. However, like many traditional social clubs, it faced challenges in maintaining membership and financial sustainability in later years. Ultimately, the Burbage Liberal Club closed its doors in 2007, marking the end of an era for this historic institution.

Following its closure, the building was converted into a SPAR convenience store, later to host the relocated Post Office services from Church Street. The history of the Burbage Liberal Club reflects the changing nature of community spaces, showcasing their evolution to remain relevant to the needs of the people they serve.

The Liberal club was a close community and during WW1 and WW2 held fund raising and support events for those fighting in the wars and supporting their families. After the War the club placed two frames on the walls of the club. The first showing the pictures and names of those from the club that had lost their lives in WW2. The second a Roll of Honour for those members of the club who had fought in the conflict. The names and photographs on this commemorative frame are; L.D. Jones, B Thatcher, V Davis, S Comer, and W. Nickerson. The photograph of Pte Peter Thomas Kavanagh is also displayed. Peter is the son of Alfred and May Kavanagh; husband of Evelyn Kavanagh, of Burbage, Leicestershire. He was killed on the 2nd September 1944 in Italy. Both frames are now in the custody of the Hinckley & District Museum.

Figure 238 Burbage Liberal Club Memorial Board to WW2 fallen.

Figure 239 Burbage Liberal Club - Roll of Honour those members of the club who Served in WW2 (Transcript below).

Allcoat T		Hollins F	Longslowe G		Wells W
Alsop S		Herbert E			Wood R
Ashby D	Davis V C	Hoyle A		Robinson C	Wright F
Atkins G	Dowell A	Hoden E	Mayne S	Robinson T	Wyles W
	Dowell R	Hughes F	Makepeace J	Rowley D	Ward C W
	Dowell W	Hill J	Malkin G	Rowley T	Wormleighton Joan (Miss)
		Hubbard J	Malkin B		Wheat R
			Marne A		Wood E
			Meeks L W		Wood G
Buttell M (Miss)	Elson H		Mills A L	Shilton F	Wormleighton A
Ball C		Illstone S	Mills T	Smith H	Woodward N
Bates W		Ingram J	Mitton A	Smith R	Wykes J
Baum C			Mitton S	Stevens A	Waring B
Bennett S	Farmer H		Moore L	Spencer S	Wheeler C
Brown V	Fleming A E	James S	Midgaff L	Spray C	Wyles L
Braker T	Fletcher C	James H	Moore L A	Storer F	Wightman J
Brown A H	Foy A	Jelley T			Wileman K
Buswell A S	Foxon K	Jones L	Neale F		
Buswell R	Frisby J	Jones D	Nickerson W		York A
Brown C				Tyler A	
Boot R				Tyler G	
Bradshaw A		Kavanagh P T		Townsend C	
	Garner F	Kenney R	Owen J	Thatcher A S	
Campton T	Gallard H	Kirk S		Thatcher B E	
Cannell W F	Garner J			Thompson F	
Cheney H	Gibbard G			Thompson G	
Charlton G	Ghent R		Parker J	Thompson W K	
Chamberlain S	Gibbard P	Lane K	Payne R	Truslove G	
Chippendale J W		Langham G	Pearson J		
Comer S		Langham W	Payne G		
Cooper G	Harding A	List L	Parker W		
Cox A	Hanson D	Lea G	Powers W		
Cox E	Haddon L	Lewis H	Powers H		
Cope W A	Hague C	Lewis R	Pratt G		
Cooper F	Harvey H	Lord G	Powell F		
Chamberlain B	Hall H	Lord J	Pritchard J		
Cliff P (Miss)	Handley J W	Lord W			Fallen in Red

Regent Club Hinckley

The Regent Club in Rugby Road, Hinckley was built in 1928/9 as a social club with a billiard room, smoke room, concert hall and other small rooms. After WW2 a fine memorial was erected at the club to commemorate those members who had lost their lives in the war.

After the club closed and the building repurposed, the memorial was saved from the scrap metal merchant and offered to Hinckley Museum. Unable to display the memorial at the museum it was passed to the care of the Leicester War Memorials at Risk Project. Founded in 2012 this wonderful project seeks to rescue war memorials at risk of loss or damage from closed or deserted buildings e.g. churches, factories, clubs or schools. The memorial can currently be viewed at their open days in the Chancel of All Saints' Church, Leicester. The names of the Burbage fallen recorded on this memorial are Dennis S. Comer and Kenneth R. Lockton.

Figure 240 Regent Club, Hinckley - Memorial to WW2.

BURBAGE AT WAR

War is Declared

For Burbage, like the rest of the country there was an immediate impact on daily life after the declaration of war in September 1939. Six days later, the weekly newspaper the Hinckley Times announced that Air Raid Precautions (ARP) units had been set up. The seriousness of the situation was brought home to local folk when Birmingham evacuees began to stream into the district. During wartime windows were ordered to be covered 'blacked out' to minimise artificial light and prevent enemy aircraft from identifying targets. Shops were "raided" for materials to darken windows for the blackout and they sold out in record time.

The paper noted that, by the end of the week, the town was as well blacked out, as any area. White lines were painted down the middle of roads, to reduce accidents, air raid shelters were being built, policemen had started using "full war kit" which included tin hats, this sight prompted double takes from residents. Football and sport were cancelled and cinemas closed. The Regent and Odeon kept their staff on standby until they could reopen. In Burbage the 1939 Armistice Parade was cancelled, but a special service was held by Reverend Pughe in the Parish Church and other services were held in the village Chapels.

Burbage Firemen

During the Second World War, the village's Reserve Firemen played a crucial role in safeguarding communities from the devastating effects of air raids and other wartime emergencies. These individuals, often volunteers or part-time workers, were responsible for responding to fires caused by bombings, ensuring the safety of residents and protecting vital infrastructure. Working with limited resources, they used water pumps, hoses, and basic equipment to combat blazes, often risking their lives in dangerous and unpredictable conditions. Village firemen also contributed to civil defence efforts, assisting with evacuations and providing support to other emergency services. Their bravery and dedication exemplified community resilience during the war, ensuring the safety and stability of rural areas in the face of significant challenges.

Figure 241 Burbage Reserve Fireman.

Land Girls

The Women's Land Army, famously known as the Land Girls, was established in 1939 during the Second World War to address labour shortages in agriculture as men joined the armed forces. These women, often from urban areas, took on physically demanding farm work, such as ploughing fields, harvesting crops, and tending to livestock, ensuring Britain's food supply during a time of crisis. They were instrumental in boosting wartime food production and reducing reliance on imports, which were severely limited due to enemy blockades. Despite facing initial scepticism and challenging conditions, the Land Girls earned respect for their dedication, adaptability, and contribution to the war effort. Their role highlighted women's capability and resilience, paving the way for broader societal changes post-war.

Figure 242 A group of local 'Land Girls'.

Blackouts

With the light pollution experienced today, it is difficult for us to understand the full impact of the Black-out on day-to-day life during the war. In September 1941 at about ten-thirty in the evening just outside the Anchor, in Church Street, John Jones a 76 year-old pensioner was hit by a passing bus and killed. The inquest recorded a very common phrase in reports of the time, *"the driver did not stand a chance of avoiding the collision"*.

Man Killed in Black-out at Burbage

ACCIDENT WHICH SHOULD "NEVER HAVE HAPPENED"

A Burbage man was fatally injured by a Midland Red 'bus just outside the Anchor Inn, Church St., Burbage, shortly before ten o'clock on Staurday night. He died before reaching Hinckley and District Hospital.

Figure 243 Hinckley Times 26th September 1941.

Only a few months later, just eleven days into the new year of 1942, on Sunday 11th January, Mr John Malkin of Sketchley Road Burbage was walking along Rugby Road at the top of Sketchley Hill when he was knocked down by a car which failed to stop. He was taken to Hinckley District Hospital for treatment. He died the next day due to the injuries he sustained, without regaining consciousness. His death was a shock to his family and many in the village, as he was well known locally. His brother, Percy Malkin lost his life in the First World War, having been awarded the Military Medal, and John's death was a further blow to the family. A police appeal for information was broadcast nationally on the BBC, after the 6 o'clock news.

BLACK-OUT FATALITY

Burbage Man Knocked Down by Unknown Car

While walking home from Hinckley on Sunday night, John Malkin, aged 33, a firewatcher, of 191, Sketchley Road, Burbage, was knocked down by a car on the Wolvey side of Sketchley Hill, and sustained injuries from which he died in Hinckley and District Hospital the folling night.

Malkin was a member of a well-known Burbage family, and the news of his death came as a shock to all who knew him.

He had left home about six o'clock on Sunday night to go to Hinckley, and it was while returning home that he was knocked down by a car, the driver of which, it is stated, failed to stop.

POLICE SEARCH FOR CAR

Inquiries were immediately made throughtout a wide area in an effort to trace the driver and a police mes- was broadcast by the B.B.C. after the six o'clock news on Tuesday

Earlier in the day the police had issued the following statement to the Press:

"At about 10.30 p.m. on Sunday last, 11th January, a man was walking from Hinckley to Burbage, and when at the top of Sketchley Hill, he was knocked down by a saloon car travelling from Hinckley towards Coventry. He received injuries from which he has since died. The car concerned did not stop. The Hinckley police request that the driver of the car or any witness of the accident should communicate with them immediately. A small plated motor-car side lamp was found at the scene of the accident."

Figure 244 Hinckley Times 16th January 1942.

Hinckley & Burbage Houses Bombed

A bomb made a large crater in the gardens of some homes in the housing estate of a Midland town, but in the circumstances there was surprisingly little damage. It fell between the Anderson shelters and the houses, wrecking three houses, and shattering two others, but other houses close by escaped without even a broken pane of glass. It was there that Mrs. Peake lost her life.

Midland Raid Victims: Homes Wrecked

Figure 245 Leicester Daily Mercury 17th May 1941.

Figure 246 Number 1 & 2 Flamville Road Burbage.

The Midlands endured significant hardship during the bomber raids of 1940/41, a critical period in the Second World War. As an industrial hub, the region was a prime target for the German Luftwaffe, which sought to disrupt Britain's manufacturing capabilities. Cities such as Coventry and Birmingham suffered devastating air raids, with factories, homes, and infrastructure reduced to rubble. The Coventry Blitz in November 1940, followed by continued attacks into 1941, caused widespread destruction and loss of life, leaving communities in shock.

Here in Burbage the distant night sky of the 14th November 1940 was visibly red from the fires caused by the devastation occurring in Coventry. The air raid on the city that night was the single most concentrated attack on a British city in the War.

Despite this, the people across the Midlands demonstrated remarkable resilience. Local efforts focused on rebuilding and maintaining production, ensuring that munitions, aircraft, and machinery essential to the war effort continued to flow, symbolising the nation's unwavering resolve.

German bombing across the country, including the Midlands, continued during the Spring of 1941. As Easter approached, further bombing occurred in Coventry. *The Times of London*, recorded; "a doctor, three sisters, two nurses, and several patients were killed when a hospital in Coventry was battered by both high explosives and fire bombs". One of those patients was Mr Sidney Shaw of Burbage, see page 60.

On the night of the 16th/17th of May Hinckley and Burbage suffered bomb damage, with four men, six women and one child being killed in Merevale Avenue. Newspaper reporting did not identify the location, but a report on the 17th May in the Leicester Daily Mercury captures the events that night at a 'Midland Town', see Figure 245. The same night, in Burbage, houses were badly damaged in Flamville Road, see Figure 246, and a large bomb crater left near Lord's Lane (now known as Aston Lane).

DOUBLE ATTACK ON COVENTRY

HOSPITAL PATIENTS AND NURSES KILLED

Five of the six successes by fighter pilots on Tuesday night belong to one Fighter Command Station, and four of the five to one squadron. A flight commander of this squadron has recently been decorated by the King. He gained his first night success and brought his total to date to 13½.

The fifth success for the station was obtained by a New Zealand D.F.C. squadron leader who was a survivor from H.M.S. Glorious.

Coventry was the Germans' main objective on Tuesday night, and it had a heavy double attack in which high-explosives and incendiaries were rained down, causing numerous casualties and considerable damage.

A doctor three sisters. two nurses and several patients were killed when a hospital in Coventry was battered by both high explosives and fire bombs. When one of the first bombs fell Joyce Miles, a nurse, was sheltering beneath a bed with a patient, and both had lucky escapes when they fell through the floor. Nurse Miles immediately went to help other injured patients, though her hands were bleeding and her clothes torn to shreds. Other nurses were injured, but the matron said that within a few minutes all were carrying out their duties.

Nine people and a child of seven were killed and a number of people injured in a raid over a south coast town. Rescue work, which went on all through the night, was still proceeding yesterday in one area where four houses were demolished. Three persons were found dead at a skating rink which was hit, and 15 people who had been trapped were rescued.

Figure 247 The Times 10th April 1941.

Figure 248 Burbage Fireman inspect a crater left by a bomb in a field near Lord's Lane.

The Barracks

In 1940 the old Moore Eady and Murcott Goode factory, in Burbage, was commissioned as a Barracks for troops.

The hosiery company also had a factory in Hinckley which is now the Concordia Theatre. Their factories were known as the '*Britannia Works*', named after the company's trading brand 'Britianna'. Britannia Road which runs alongside the old factory was originally called '*Balls Lane*' after a landowner in the area. The renamed lane evidently took its name from the old factory.

Shown below are the first occupants - the Royal Army Medical Corps, photographed nearby.

In February 1944 the American 307th Airborne Engineers were based at the old factory prior to the preparations for the invasion of France later in the year, see page 109.

After the war the building was used for a number of years as a Territorial Army (TA) Training Centre. After the TA vacated the building, during much of the 1960s and 1970s the building would stand unused.

Today in 2025 it is good to see the building back in-use as individual commercial units.

Figure 249 The Old Factory at the top of Britannia Road, known as 'The Barracks' photographed c1950.

Figure 250 Royal Army Medical Corps Photographed in Burbage.

Home Guard

The Home Guard, often referred to as "*Dad's Army*", was formed in 1940 during the Second World War to defend Britain from the threat of German invasion. Comprising volunteers ineligible for regular military service, including older men, younger boys, and those in reserved occupations, the Home Guard became a vital component of Britain's defence strategy. Their duties included manning checkpoints, patrolling key infrastructure, and preparing for potential enemy landings. Despite limited initial training and equipment, the volunteers demonstrated determination and ingenuity, adapting to the challenges of their role. The Home Guard not only bolstered Britain's defences but also boosted national morale, symbolising community spirit and resilience during a time of immense uncertainty and danger.

Burbage like other villages had their own platoon of Home Guard. A large number of these men were veterans of WW1.

(No. 9)
Burbage photograph taken at Dr. Donovan's Surgery on the Lawn. Back Row: ——, Mr. Malkin, ——, ——, ——, Mr. Taylor, Mr. Grant, ——, ——, Mr. Atkins, ——, Mr. Foxon. Second Row: Mr. Rowe, ——, ——, ——, Mr. Hollier, ——, ——, ——, Mr. Woodward, Mr. Mabletoft, Mr. Green, Mr. Aldridge. Third Row: ——, Mr. Colkin, ——, Mr. Cross, Mr. Nichols, ——, Mr. Nichols, ——, ——, Mr. Mason, Mr. Waring, Mr. Lord, ——. Front Row: Mr. Harrison, ——, Mr. Ghent, Mr. Wormleton, Mr. Robinson, Mr. Flude, Mr. Harding, ——, Mr. Greenaway, Mr. Thorn, ——, Mr. Collinson. Some names are missing. The Author would be pleased to hear from anyone knowing these.

Figure 251 Burbage Home Guard Newspaper Photograph.

Co-op Hall

Local dances during the Second World War provided a significant morale boost to communities across Britain, offering a much-needed escape from the hardships of war. Held in village halls, community centres, and air raid shelters, these gatherings brought people together to enjoy music, camaraderie, and a sense of normality amidst the chaos. Dances often featured live bands or gramophone music, with popular styles like swing and jazz lifting spirits and encouraging social interaction. For service members on leave, dances were a chance to relax and connect with loved ones, while civilians found comfort in shared moments of joy. These events fostered community resilience, strengthened bonds, and reminded participants of the enduring importance of unity and hope during challenging times.

In Burbage the Co-operative Hall was the prime location for these dances, with reduced prices being quoted for troops. As another advertisement in the next column shows the hall took many roles, on 3rd Oct hosting the Sunday services.

In 2025, the hall is still in the ownership of the Central Co-op, although it has now been converted into flats.

St. Catherine's Church BURBAGE

Sunday, October 3rd
CHURCH CLOSED FOR REPAIRS
Services:
CO-OPERATIVE HALL
11-0 a.m. and 6-0 p.m.

Figure 252 1921 Hinckley Times 1st October 1943

Leicester Royal Infirmary

BURBAGE CO-OP. HALL
DANCE
Saturday, October 2nd
TED COLLIS and his BAND
7.30 p.m. - 11.30 p.m.
ADMISSION 2/-. TROOPS 1/-

Figure 253 1921 Hinckley Times 1st October 1943

Figure 254 Co-operative Hall, Burbage.

Burbage Spitfire

During the Second World War, public fundraising campaigns across Britain played a significant role in financing the production of the iconic Spitfire fighter aircraft. Communities, organisations, and individuals enthusiastically participated in "Spitfire Funds," donating money to support the Royal Air Force in its efforts to defend the nation. Fundraising initiatives ranged from charity events, raffles, and auctions to more creative endeavours, such as sponsored activities and collections at workplaces. Each Spitfire cost approximately £5,000, a substantial sum at the time, and many planes were named after the towns, cities, or groups that contributed to their purchase. These campaigns not only bolstered the RAF's capabilities but also fostered a sense of unity and determination among the British public during the war.

Public support for the war is recognised by donations from the local area to purchase new planes for the war effort. May 1941 sees a new Spitfire Commissioned, which bears the name "Burbage"

The war very quickly establishes some brave and successful fighter pilots. One such pilot is John Colin Mungo-Park (DFC). On the evening of the twenty-seventh of June, flying spitfire VB X4668, he was shot down and killed just north of Dunkirk. Sadly, spitfire X4668 was the plane named, "Burbage".

The Burbage Spitfire

Figure 255 Spitfire VB X4668 – Burbage Spitfire.

Dam Buster - Geoff Rice

The famous story of the bouncing bomb and the plan to inflict a blow to German industry, by breeching the Ruhr Valley dams has a Burbage connection.

In 1943, the RAF, 617 squadron carried out a critical operation, Operation Chastise. In total, 19 Lancaster Bombers flew from RAF Scampton to Germany, in three formations. Aircraft call sign H for Harry was flown by Burbage commander Geoffrey Rice DFC (1917-81).

Of the 19 aircraft which flew, only eleven would return to base, including Geoff Rice who returned after clipping the sea on the outbound flight and losing the mine.

Whatever the result of the nineteen sorties, each and every member of all the crews played their role in this brave mission.

Of course, as the radio reports announcing the raid were heard here in the village, nobody would have any knowledge of the role Geoff Rice had played in the attack. But it is fitting the he is now acknowledged by a plaque, on what was once his Grandparents house, the Sycamores Inn.

Figure 256 Geoffrey Rice DFC 1917-81
617 'Dam Buster' Squadron.

Figure 257 The Sycamores Inn Showing Plaques to Geoffrey Rice DFC and the 307th Airbourne Engineers.

Peace

Victory in Europe May 1945

Figure 258 VE Day Celebrations Windsor Street, (Rear of The Bull's Head, 34 Windsor Street)

Victory in Europe Day (VE Day), celebrated on 8th May 1945, marked the official end of World War II in Europe. It commemorated the unconditional surrender of Nazi Germany's armed forces to the Allied powers, bringing an end to nearly six years of devastating conflict across the continent.

The surrender was formally signed on 7th May in Reims, France, and came into effect the following day. This historic moment followed the suicide of Adolf Hitler on 30th April 1945, and the rapid advance of Allied forces through Germany. While the war in the Pacific against Japan continued, VE Day represented a significant milestone in the path toward global peace.

Across Europe and North America, people poured into the streets to celebrate. Cities like London, Paris, and New York erupted with jubilation, with crowds waving flags, singing, and embracing the hard-won victory. In Britain, Prime Minister Winston Churchill addressed the nation, and King George VI made a rare radio broadcast to share the news.

Despite the celebrations, VE Day was also a moment of reflection. Millions had perished, cities lay in ruins, and the enormity of rebuilding and addressing the war's atrocities loomed. Still, VE Day symbolised hope and a new beginning after a time of unimaginable hardship.

YOUNG AND OLD CELEBRATE AT BURBAGE

In Windsor Street, Burbage, VE-Day was celebrated with a tea for children and the old people, at which 161 sat down, in addition to the helpers and others who sat down later, the total party numbering 241. Later sports and races were arranged in the street for which prizes were given, and the food that remained after everybody had fed plentifully was auctioned by Mr Gordon Bailey, and the sum of £8 12s. 6d. was raised and forwarded to the funds of the Red Cross. Subsequently there were games and dancing in the street until midnight. Mrs Parkes, aged 70, sang solos and played the piano (taken from one of the inns), and songs were also rendered by Master J. Baker.

Figure 259 Hinckley Times 18th May 1945

Victory in Japan August 1945

Victory over Japan Day (VJ Day), observed on 15th August 1945, marked the end of World War II following Japan's surrender. This historic moment came after years of brutal conflict in the Pacific and the devastating atomic bombings of Hiroshima (6th August) and Nagasaki (9th August), which led to massive destruction and loss of life.

Japan announced its surrender on 15th August 1945, following Emperor Hirohito's radio address, in which he urged his people to accept defeat to prevent further suffering. The formal surrender ceremony took place on 2nd September 1945, aboard the USS Missouri in Tokyo Bay, with representatives from Japan and the Allied powers, including General Douglas MacArthur.

VJ Day was met with enormous celebrations worldwide. In cities such as New York, London, and Sydney, euphoric crowds filled the streets, waving flags and embracing the end of a war that had claimed tens of millions of lives. The iconic photograph of a sailor kissing a nurse in Times Square captured the joy and relief felt by many.

While VJ Day marked the end of the conflict, it also brought reflection on the immense cost of war, the challenges of rebuilding, and the hope for a lasting peace in a world forever changed by World War II.

The announcement of the Japanese surrender became known in Britan late at night on the 14th August, with the surrender intended to start at midnight. The late hour of the announcement left many asleep, unaware of the end of war, until they arrived at work the following morning, only to find that a holiday had been announced. Two days of public holiday were declared by the government. In some newspapers these days were referred to as VJ Day & VJ Day+1.

The Leicester Evening Mail reported on the evening of the 15th that fighting continued in Burma whilst the British Commanders waited to be satisfied that the Japanese in Burma had fully accepted the surrender. It was estimated that between 50,000 and 60,000 Japanese would surrender in Burma.

In London, rain-soaked crowds greeted the King's procession to open Parliament. The paper notes that VE Day crowds were small in comparison with the host of VJ Day jubilant celebrators.

In Burbage the newspaper reported that Wednesday's celebrations are limited, but the Hinckley Times reported that St Catherine's church was floodlit in celebration and The Rev Pughe held a special service at the Church. Services of thanksgiving were also held at the Methodist and Congregational Churches.

A number of street parties were held across Burbage which are said to have surpassed those of VE day.

Figure 260 Hinckley Times 17th August 1945

HAPPY CROWDS AT BARWELL, BURBAGE AND EARL SHILTON

LUTTERWORTH ROAD, BURBAGE

Lutterworth Road, Burbage, provided excellent tea and celebrations for the children, thanks to the generosity of the residents. In fact there was more than enough, and surplus goods were afterwards auctioned off, £7 being realised for Hinckley and District Hospital. Later on, to conclude the celebrations, the children are being given an outing to Wicksteed Park.

BURBAGE CHILDREN AT WICKSTEED

Children living on the Three Pots Estate, Burbage, celebrated in a novel way, journeying by 'bus to Wicksteed Park. Altogether three 'bus loads, including a number of parents, made the journey, and on arrival at the Park a substantial tea was provided and games played. Each child was given 2/- spending money together with a bar of chocolate and minerals. It was a tired but happy band of children that arrived home shortly before dusk.

PROF. PAYNE AND "JOEY" AT BURBAGE PARTY

The children living in Upper Windsor Street, Burbage, had a great time. Thanks to the efforts of Mrs. S. Shilton, and an energetic committee excellent arrangements were made to ensure everyone being happy. The celebrations took place on a big lawn in, what is known as, Barrack Yard, where a splendid tea was served followed by games and dancing and an entertainment given by Prof. W. E. Payne, assisted by the ever-popular "Joey." Mr. Payne's conjuring mystified everyone and "Joey" made them laugh until they cried. At night a huge bonfore was lighted and the festivities were kept up until the fire went out.

Figure 261 Hinckley Times 24th & 31st August 1945

THREE DAYS' CELEBRATIONS IN SAPCOTE ROAD

In Sapcote Road about fifty children were treated to a sumptuous tea last Thursday, after which there were sports and games in a nearby field, prizes being given to the lucky competitors. Celebrations lasted over three days. On Wednesday night there was a bonfire, and roast potatoes and toffee apples provided for the children. The next evening there was another bonfire, and a display of fireworks. Supper was partaken of sitting round the fire, and sweets, fruit and ice cream provided for the children. On Staurday the children took part in a fancy dress parade, and supper was again served round a hugh bonfire. With the funds still in hand it is hoped to provide an outing to Wicksteed Park.

OPEN AIR PARTIES AT BURBAGE

There were victory teas in practically every street in Burbage. The children of Hinckley Road sat down to a spread which surpassed, if possible, the one held on VE day. The children and adults were in high spirits and there were more on the tables that even the youthful and adult appetites could master. Afterwards there was singing and dancing.

In Sketchley Road there were three parties. In the lower part of the road children and parents joined in a tea and sing-song and on the front lawn of one of the resident's the grown-ups showed how they could celebrate. They sat down to a wonderful tea and then joined a community singing of all the old-time favourites the Festivities being kept up until darkness fell. The children living higher up the road had an open-air tea at the entrance to one of the houses and did full justice to the good things provided and then adjourned to a field known as the Cow Pastures for games. The funds had been so generously subscribed that each child was given 3/6 and a bar of chocolate.

British Colonial Areas in the Far East

The British colonial presence in Asia would have a significant impact on a number of Burbage soldiers in a region which even prior to WW2 was experiencing tensions and change. Countries saw significant geopolitical shifts due to colonialism, imperial expansion, and post-war decolonisation. The region experienced border changes, gained independence, or underwent name changes during this key period of the 20th century. Below is an overview of the key changes:

Burma

Pre-War

In the period before WW2 Burma was under British colonial rule, initially administered as a province of British India. The period was marked by significant political and social changes, driven by rising nationalist sentiments among the Burmese populace. In 1920, the General Council of Burmese Associations (GCBA) was established by nationalists, to advocate for Burmese interests. The GCBA's People's Party faction won 28 out of 58 contested seats in the 1922 Legislative Council elections. The 1930s saw increased political activity which played a pivotal role in mobilizing anti-colonial sentiment. In 1937, the British government separated Burma from India, granting it a new constitution and limited self-governance. Despite these reforms, tensions persisted, leading to events like the 1938 Anti-Indian & Anti-Muslim riots, which highlighted underlying social and economic disparities. Throughout this era, Burma's governance evolved from direct colonial administration to a form of limited self-rule, setting the stage for the country's eventual push toward full independence.

During WWII:

Burma was occupied by Japan.

Post-War Changes:

Burma gained independence from Britain in 1948 and was renamed Myanmar in 1989.

Malaysia and Singapore

Pre-War

In the period before WW2 Singapore was a British Crown Colony, serving as the capital of the Straits Settlements. The colonial government was led by a British-appointed governor, supported by the Legislative Council, which primarily comprised officials and nominated members, with limited local representation. During this period, the government focused on urban development and public health. In 1927, the Singapore Improvement Trust (SIT) was established to address urban planning, housing, and infrastructure needs. The colonial administration was cautious about political participation among locals. A 1920 select committee argued that Singapore was not ready for democratic reforms, fearing that elections might enable "professional politicians" to exploit social divisions. Consequently, the Legislative Council remained largely under British control, with limited input from the local populace. The government was also vigilant against anti-colonial activities. Despite these challenges, Singapore's strategic location ensured its continued prosperity as a trading hub. The population grew, and the city expanded its financial institutions, communications, and infrastructure to support booming trade and industry.

During WWII:

Singapore was occupied by Japan.

Post-War Changes:

These countries gained independence from Britain in stages: Malaya (1957), later forming Malaysia (1963) with Sabah, Sarawak, and Singapore. Singapore became independent in 1965.

Thailand

Pre-War

In the period before WW2 Thailand was known as Siam. In this period, it underwent significant political transformation. King Prajadhipok (Rama VII) ascended the throne in 1925, inheriting a nation grappling with economic challenges exacerbated by the global Great Depression. The economic downturn led to plummeting rice prices and widespread financial hardship, particularly among the urban middle class and state employees in Bangkok. Dissatisfaction grew among a group of Western-educated students and military officers who were frustrated with the absolute monarchy's tight political control. In 1932, The People's Party orchestrated a bloodless coup, effectively ending the absolute monarchy and ushering in a constitutional government. Following the coup, the new government introduced a provisional constitution, marking Thailand's shift towards constitutional monarchy. King Prajadhipok remained as a symbolic figurehead, but real political power transitioned to the People's Party leaders. This period saw the drafting of Thailand's first permanent constitution in 1932, which aimed to establish a parliamentary system. However, political instability persisted, characterized by internal conflicts and power struggles within the new government. In 1935, King Prajadhipok abdicated, expressing disillusionment with the political developments. He was succeeded by his nephew, Ananda Mahidol (Rama VIII), who was then studying abroad. The young king's absence led to increased military influence in governance. By the late 1930s, military figures rose to prominence, steering Thailand towards a more authoritarian regime. This period for Siam, marked by the transition from absolute monarchy to constitutional governance, significant political upheaval, and the emergence of military dominance in the nation's political landscape. In 1939, the country officially changed its name from Siam to Thailand, meaning "Land of the Free," to reflect its independence and the unity of the Thai people.

During WWII
Thailand was never colonised by a European power, which sets it apart from its neighbours. In 1941, Thailand signed an alliance with Imperial Japan, allowing Japanese forces to use Thai territory as a base for their campaigns in Southeast Asia. While the Thai government, aligned with Japan, there was internal resistance. The Free Thai Movement (Seri Thai), supported by the Allies, worked against Japanese control from within. During the war, Thailand temporarily expanded its territory by annexing parts of French Indochina (modern-day Laos and Cambodia) with Japanese support.

Post-War Changes
After Japan's defeat, Thailand was forced to return these territories to French control as part of the peace settlements. The name briefly reverted to Siam from 1945 to 1949 before becoming Thailand again, which it remains today. Thailand escaped harsh punishment for its wartime alliance with Japan by shifting allegiance to the Allies before the war ended. This helped Thailand maintain its sovereignty and avoid occupation or division like many other nations in the region. Thailand's borders are largely unchanged since WWII. Its avoidance of colonisation, along with its strategic manoeuvring during and after the war, allowed it to emerge relatively stable compared to its neighbours.

India, Pakistan & Bangladesh
Pre-War
In the period before WW2 India (which included the areas now known as Pakistan & Bangladesh) was under British colonial rule, experiencing significant political transformations and growing nationalist movements. The Government of India Act of 1919 introduced limited self-governance, establishing a dyarchy system that divided powers between British officials and Indian ministers in provincial governments. However, this arrangement fell short of Indian aspirations for full self-rule. In response, the Indian National Congress (INC), launched the Non-Cooperation Movement in 1920, advocating for non-violent resistance against British policies. This movement saw widespread boycotts of British goods, institutions, and honours. Although it was suspended in 1922 following violent incidents, it marked a significant escalation in the push for independence. The Simon Commission of 1928, established to assess India's readiness for further self-governance, faced widespread opposition due to its all-British composition. The British government's rejection of dominion status for India proposals led to the Civil Disobedience Movement in 1930. The Government of India Act of 1935 was a significant legislative reform, introducing provincial autonomy and proposing the establishment of a federal structure. While it granted more powers to Indian representatives at the provincial level, the central government remained under British control. This act laid the groundwork for India's eventual self-governance. Throughout this period, India's political landscape was characterized by a growing demand for independence, marked by mass mobilisations, legislative reforms, and an evolving struggle between colonial authorities and nationalist leaders.

During WW2
The country remained a British colony during the war and played a critical role in the Allied war effort, contributing over 2.5 million soldiers, one of the largest volunteer armies.

Post-War Changes
India gained independence from Britain in 1947, but this came at a heavy cost: the Partition of British India into two separate states; Dominion of India (later Republic of India) and Dominion of Pakistan. This division was based largely on religious lines, with India predominantly Hindu and Pakistan predominantly Muslim. The new borders were drawn by the Radcliffe Line, dividing Punjab and Bengal between India and Pakistan. Massive violence and population displacement followed, with millions migrating across the new borders. In 1971 East Pakistan seceded from Pakistan after a bloody conflict, with Indian military support. This led to the creation of Bangladesh. In 1975 the Himalayan kingdom of Sikkim became a part of India after a referendum, becoming the 22nd state.

INDEX

Aeroplanes
- Harvard Trainer ... 47
- Hawker Hurricanes ... 47
- Tiger Moth ... 47
- Wellington Bomber ... 103, 108, 114, 115

American Army Units
- 101st Airbourne ... 57
- 307th Airborne Engineers ... 109, 113, 128
- 376th Parachute Field Artillery ... 109
- 82nd Airborne ... 57, 109, 111

Battles
- Belgium, Ardennes ... 23
- Burma
  - Arakan Peninsula ... 94
  - Meiktila ... 96
  - Myitkyina ... 42
- Egypt
  - El Alamein ... 35
  - Medenine ... 35
- France
  - Gold Beach ... 52
  - St Desir ... 52
  - St Mere Eglise ... 113
- Italy
  - Ancona to Rimini ... 29
  - Anzio ... 18, 58
  - Coriano Ridge ... 79
  - Gustav Line ... 18, 58
- Libya, Siege of Tobruk ... 73
- Malaya
  - Kota Bharu ... 63
- Netherlands, Nijmegen ... 23
- Tunisia
  - Enfidaville ... 45, 87
  - Mareth Line ... 87

British Army Regiments
- 4th Queen's Own Hussars ... 89
- Bedfordshire ... 37, 92
- Chindits Force ... 41
- Hampshire ... 29
- Leicestershire ... 21, 29, 41, 44, 51, 63, 83
- Leicestershire Yeomanry ... 33
- Northamptonshire ... 18, 27, 96
- Royal Army Medical Corps ... 128
- Royal Army Ordnance Corps ... 73
- Royal Army Service Corps ... 23, 25, 26, 56
- Royal Artillery ... 87
- Royal Berkshire ... 83
- Royal Engineers ... 32, 33, 34
- Royal Inniskilling ... 94
- Sherwood Forresters ... 73, 79
- The Queens Royal ... 58

British Legion
- Burbage ... 12, 61, 105
- National ... 12, 97

Burbage Fallen of the Great War (Book) ... 8
Burbage Heritage Group ... 109, 129

Burbage Locations
- Anchor Inn, Church Street ... 125
- Balls Lane (now Britannia Road) ... 39, 128
- Brockhurst Avenue ... 61, 114
- Burbage Hall ... 109
- Canning House, Church Street ... 25
- Church Street ... 10, 25
- Constitutional Club, Church Street ... 25, 96
- Co-operative Hall ... 11, 112, 130
- Coventry Road ... 41, 67
- Featherston Drive ... 105
- Flamville Road ... 37, 50, 81, 83, 127
- Freemans Lane ... 89, 92
- Hinckley Knight ... 109
- Hinckley Road ... 25
- Holt Farm ... 104
- Liberal Club, Lutterworth Road ... 29, 121
- Lord's Lane (now Aston Lane) ... 127
- Lutterworth Road ... 41, 44, 51, 73, 79, 108
- Lychgate Lane ... 44, 47, 58, 76
- Memorial Garden (Proposed) ... 11
- Mickle Hill ... 108
- Orchard Farm ... 108
- Salem Road ... 63
- Sapcote Road ... 94
- Sketchley Hill ... 66, 125
- Sketchley Road ... 87, 125
- Strutt Road ... 18, 34
- The Barracks ... 109, 128
- The Green ... 10
- The Horsepool ... 56
- The Sycamores Inn ... 113, 131, 132
- Watling Street ... 27
- Windsor Street ... 34, 92
- Woodland Avenue ... 21

Cause of Death
- Aeroplane Crash ... 48
- Air Raid ... 81
- Battle Combat .. 18, 23, 26, 27, 35, 44, 52, 54, 56, 58, 79, 84, 94
- Cancer ... 66, 76
- Enemy Action whilst on Bomb Disposal Duty ... 33
- Fever ... 41
- Flying Accident ... 47
- Friendly Fire (POW) ... 68
- Lost Overboard ... 39
- POW ... 63, 89, 92
- Road Accident ... 61
- Sniper ... 96
- Unknown Illness ... 71, 73

Cemeteries
- Aston Flamville, St Peter's Churchyard ... 71
- Burbage, St Catherine's Churchyard ... 47, 48, 62, 73
- Coventry, London Road ... 81
- Hinckley Cemetery ... 66
- Montgomery USA, Oakwood ... 75, 76, 77
- Sutton Bridge Churchyard ... 48

Index

Churches & Chapels
    Aston Flamville, St Peter's 116
    Burbage
        Congregational 118
        St Catherine's 61, 124, 134
        Wesleyan 96, 110, 117
    Hinckley
        Holy Trinity Church 66
        St Peter's Roman Catholic 112, 119
    Leicester, All Saints' Church 123
    Lincoln, St Paul-in-the-Bail's 83
    Ryton, Methodist Church 51
Commanding Officers
    Lloyd, Mjr Gen WL 94
    Morrison, Lt-Col Charles Esmond 63
    Percival, Lt Gen Arthur 101
Events of WW2
    Coventry Blitz 81, 127
    Dunkirk Evacuation 26, 35, 73
    Hinckley & Burbage Bomb Damage 127
    Invasion of Italy 58, 79
    Invasion of Poland 37
    Midlands Bomber Raids 1940/41 127
    Normandy Landings 57
    Operation Chastise (Dam Busters) 131
    Operation Market Garden 56, 57, 109, 113
    Operation Overlord (D-Day) 21, 109
    Pearl Harbour Attack 63, 100
    The Long March 89, 91
    Victory in Europe Day (VE Day) 133
    Victory over Japan Day (VJ Day) 134
    Wellington Bomber Crash MF-116 103
    Wellington Bomber Crash X9953 108
Hinckley Locations
    Clarendon Road 63
    Concordia Theatre 128
    District Hospital 125
    Edward Street 27
    Hinckley District Museum 113, 121
    London Road 54, 56
    Merevale Avenue 127
    Police Station, Stockwell Head 87
    Regent Club, Rugby Road 123
    Southfield Road 37, 63
    Station Road 47
    Strathmore Road 34
    Thirlmere Road 35
    Working Men's Club 110
Hinckley Urban District Council 13, 32, 87
Illness & Disease
    Cancer 66, 76
    Dysentery 41
    Malaria 41
    Malnutrition 92
Individuals Mentioned
    Allcoat, T 122
    Allen, Henry 48
    Alsop, S 122
    Ashby, D 122
    Atkins, G 122
    Ball, C 122
    Bates, W 122
    Baum, C 122
    Bayley, Don 105

Bennett, S 122
Bewicke-Copley, Robert Godfrey Wolsey (Lord Cromwell)
.... 12, 13, 14
Boot, R 122
Bradshaw, A 122
Braker, T 122
Brown, A H 122
Brown, C 122
Brown, V 122
Buswell, A S 122
Buswell, R 122
Buttell, Miss M 122
Campton, T 122
Cannell, W F 122
Chamberlain, B 122
Chamberlain, Mr A 11
Chamberlain, Mrs A 11
Chamberlain, Neville 37
Chamberlain, S 122
Chandler, Kate 117
Chapman, Pat 110
Charlton, G 122
Cheney, H 122
Chippendale, J W 122
Churchill, Winston 114, 133
Clausen, Ralph 110
Cliff, Miss P 122
Collins, Mr H 11
Cooper, G 122
Cooper, Nan Ino (Lady Lucas) 116
Cope, W A 122
Couture, Florian 110
Cox, A 122
Cox, E 122
Dowell, A 122
Dowell, R 122
Dowell, W 122
Drozdz, Greg 103, 104, 114
Drozdz, Henryk 114, 115
Dudley, Miss 25
Elson, H 122
Evans, Mr J T 11
Farmer, H 122
Farnell, Derek 112
Flavell, Mr W 92
Flavell, Mrs T 12
Fleming, A E 122
Fletcher, C 122
Foxon, K 122
Foy, A 122
Freestone, Insp John Edward 104
Frisby, J 122
Gallard, H 122
Garner, F 122
Garner, J 122
Ghent, R 122
Gibbard, G 122
Gibbard, P 122
Greenhough, Miss Elizabeth 32
Haddon, L 122
Hague, C 122
Hall, H 122
Handley, J W 122
Handley, Mr J Junr 11

139

Hanson, D	122
Harding, A	122
Harvey, H	122
Hepworth, P. D.	57
Herbert, Auberon Thomas (Lord Lucas)	116
Herbert, E	122
Higham, Stanley	25
Hill, J	122
HM King George VI	114, 133
Hoden, E	122
Hollins, F	122
Hoyle, A	122
Hubbard, J	122
Hughes, F	122
Iliffe, Mr John	11, 12
Illstone, S	122
Ingram, J	122
James, H	122
James, S	122
Jelley, T	122
Jennings, Fr David	105
Jones, D	122
Judkins, Harry	108
Kellaway, Eric	114
Kellaway, Mrs S E	11, 13
Kenney, R	122
Kew, Alan	48
Kirk, S	122
Lane, K	122
Langham, G	122
Langham, W	122
Lea, G	122
Lewis, H	122
Lewis, R	122
List, L	122
Longslowe, G	122
Lord, J	122
Lord, W	122
MacArthur, General Douglas	134
Makepeace, J	122
Malkin, B	122
Malkin, G	122
Malkin, Percy MM	125
Mansell, PO E J	108
Marne, A	122
Maufe, Sir Edward	40
Mayne, S	122
McGrah, Cllr T	11, 12
McMillan, William	40
Meeks, L W	122
Miale, Sgt Frank	109, 110, 113
Midgaff, L	122
Millar, Mr S R	11
Mills, A L	122
Mills, T	122
Mitton, A	122
Mitton, S	122
Moore, L	122
Moore, L A	122
Neale, F	122
Owen, J	122
Parker, J	122
Parker, W	122
Payne, G	122

Payne, R	122
Pearson, J	122
Petcher, Mr J	11, 12
Pinfield, Rev G E	12
Portal, Sir Charles	114
Powell, F	122
Powers, H	122
Powers, R	122
Prajadhipok, King (Thailand)	136
Pratt, G	122
Pritchard, J	122
Pudney, John	105
Pughe, Rev Richard	12, 124
Rice, Geoffrey DFC	131
Robbins, Kathleen	111
Robinson, C	122
Robinson, Mr E	11
Robinson, T	122
Rowley, D	122
Rowley, T	122
Shilton, F	122
Sikorski, General Wladyslaw	114
Simmonds, Cllr R H	12
Simpson, Brian	27
Smith, Clare	110
Smith, H	122
Smith, R	122
Soissons, Louis de	58
Spencer, S	122
Spray, C	122
Stebbeds, Sidney John	101
Stevens, A	122
Storer, F	122
Thatcher, A S	122
Thompson, F	122
Thompson, G	122
Thompson, Mr P J	12
Thompson, W K	122
Townsend, C	122
Truslove, G	122
Tyler, A	122
Tyler, G	122
Visneski, Ted	110
Ward, C W	122
Waring, B	122
Watters, Vernon	110, 113
Wells, W	122
Wheat, R	122
Wheeler, C	122
Wheeler, Charles	40
White, Mavis	110
Whitworth, Sylvia	109
Wightman, J	122
Wileman, K	122
Womack, Travis	110
Wood, E	122
Wood, G	122
Wood, R	122
Woodward, N	122
Wormleighton, A	122
Wormleighton, Miss Joan	122
Wright, F	122
Wykes, J	122
Wyles, L	122

Wyles, Michael 108
York, A 122

Lives Lost in WW2
Allen, Cpl James Frederick 18
Baer, John M 113
Barnes, Pte Charles Frank 21, 118
Billeter, Charles M 113
Carlson, Kenneth R 113
Chin, Foon G 113
Chobaniuk, FO Nicholas 103, 104, 106
Clarke, Drv Stanley 23
Colkin, Drv Edward Stanley Bernard 25
Comer, Pte Dennis 27, 118, 123
Comer, Pte Sidney Charles 29, 118, 121, 122
Connelley, John I 113
Conrad, Alfred H 113
Crump, Capt Edward Thomas 32
Cunningham, Ralph J 113
Czuhajewski, Stanley J 113
Davies, Spr Victor Charles 34, 121, 122
Dobson, Gnr Harry 37, 92, 118
Durben, Fred H 113
Durham, James I 113
Easterbrook, Earl E 113
Edmondson, Charlie K 113
Ellis, Elmer 113
Fainelli, Lawrence I 113
Felgenhauer, William W 113
Fowler, Harry G 113
Fuller, Herman R 113
Gentile, Louis F 113
Good, Sgt Leslie George 104, 106
Gunn, Sgt John Sidney 104, 106
Hadley, Ab Horace 39
Harris, Willam B 113
Harrison, Sgt George 41
Hause, Robert 113
Henschler, Edward V 113
Holyoak, Pte Frank 44, 97, 117
Howarth, Sgt Pilot Frederick John 25, 47, 117
Howkins, LCpl Frederick Harold 51, 97, 117
Hoy, Cyril 108
Jacobius, Herman I 113
Jacobs, James A 113
Jarvis, Able Seaman Percy 54
Jenkins, Willard 113
Jones, Drv Leslie David 56, 121, 122
Jones, John 125
Joseph, Horace 113
Kavanagh, Peter Thomas 121, 122
Kearns, Pte Richard Joseph 58, 119
Kellaway, Sqn Ldr Sidney Edward 60, 114
Kero, Willam E 113
King, Stanley W 113
Kreiser, Ropy K 113
Langford, Everette H 113
Letts, LCpl Harold 63, 92, 97, 117
Leverknight, Karl J 113
Lockton, AC Kenneth Bert 66, 120, 123
Lord, WO John 25, 67, 117, 120
Lount, AC1 Sidney Richard 71, 120
Lum, Emerson A 113
Malkin, John 125
Martin, William W 113
McKeeby, Benjamin I 113
McMurdo, Sgt John William 104, 106
Moore, Pte Frank 73
Mottern, Robert I 113
Mungo-Park, Sqn Ldr John Colin (DFC) 131
Murray, James 113
Nickerson, Flt Lt George William MM 75, 121, 122
O'Neill, Daniel J 113
O'Neill, John J 113
Opacich, Robert S 113
Parker, Sgt Charles Dennis 104, 107
Pritchard, Pte Francis 79
Pulliam, Ralph C 113
Rudin, George C 113
Shaw, Mr Sydney Harry 81, 127
Siddall, Elmer Q 113
Smith, Lt Thomas Frank 87, 120
Smith, Sgt George Henry 83
Souza, Moses de 113
Stephenson, James S 113
Stibor, Sgt Karel 48
Sweeney, Alexander F 113
Thatcher, Trooper Bert Edward 89, 121, 122
Thompson, Sgt John 104, 107
Tite, Gnr Jeffrey 92, 118
Tole, Carl C 113
Wendland, Herbert R 113
Wheeler, Paul D 113
White, Fusilier Walter 94
Wood, Cpl Douglas Arthur 96, 97, 117
Woods, James F 113
Wright, Preston S 113
Yeo, William W 113
Yonkin, Paul W 113

Local Roles in WW2
Air Raid Warden 87
Home Guard 76, 129
Land Girls 124
Reserve Fireman 124

Local Work Places
Ansty, Ansty Aerodrome 81
Burbage
    Burgess Products 115
    Chamberlain & Co 44
    Moore, Eady & Murcott Goode 73, 128
    Robinson's Buses 34
    Sketchley Dye Works 23, 24, 51, 96
    The Lodge, Lutterworth Road 92
Desford, Colliery 81
Hinckley
    Bennett Brothers Hosiery Man. and Dyers 37, 63
    H Flude & Co 21
    Hinckley Urban District Council 18, 56, 76
    Hospital 96
    Hunt & Co 56
    Matkins Electricians 47
    Messrs Parsons & Sherwin 47
    Midland Red 34, 54
Stoney Stanton, Messrs John Ellis & Sons 71
Warwickshire County Council 41
Wolvey, Co-operative Farm 18

Medals
- British Empire 33
- Italian Star 18
- Military Cross 12
- Military Medal 75, 125

Navy
- Merchant
  - S.S. Andes 100
- Royal 39
  - HMS Excellent II 54
- United States
  - USS Missouri 134

Occupations
- Blacksmith 44
- Bus Driver 34, 94
- Hosiery Dull Finisher 41
- Special Constable 41

Overseas Locations
- Aden 60
- Algeria 27
- Australia 27
- Bangladesh 137
- Burma (now Myanmar) 84, 94, 101, 136
- Cape Town 100
- East Pakistan .... See India
- Egypt 60, 87
- France, Reims 133
- Greece 89
- India 83, 101, 137
  - Bombay 100
- Italy 58
- Malaya 136
- Morocco 27
- Mumbai .... See Bombay
- Myanmar .... See Burma
- North Africa 35, 44
- Pakistan 137
- Poland 89
- Siam .... See Thailand
- Singapore 63, 100, 101, 136
- Suez 35
- Thailand 101, 136
  - Bangkok 136
- Trinidad 100
- Tunisia 27, 35, 54

Prisoner of War 25, 26, 67, 73, 89

Prisoner of War Camps
- Austria
  - Döllersheim 89
  - Gneixendorf 89
  - Graz 89
  - Kaisersteinbruch 89
  - Lienz 89
  - Spittal an der Drau 89
  - Wolfsberg 89
- Burma
  - Railway 92, 102
- Canary Islands
  - Interment Camp 54
- Germany 68
  - Boizenburg 68
  - Marienburg 26
- Italy
  - Campo Concentramento, Macerata 73
- Poland 68
  - Stalag 344 .... 73, 89
- Singapore
  - Selarang Barracks 101
- Thailand
  - Ban Pong 101
  - Kanburi 102

Royal Air Force 66, 75
- 617 Squadron 131
- No 18 Operational Training Unit ... 61, 114
- Polish Squadron 60, 114
- Stations
  - Bitteswell 115
  - Blandford Camp 60
  - Bramcote 61, 103, 114, 115
  - British Flying Training School in Florida, USA 76
  - Cottisford 61
  - Cranwell 71
  - Desford Training School 47
  - Eastchurch 114
  - Finningley 115
  - Nuneaton 103
  - Scampton 131
  - Sutton Bridge 47
  - Westcott 108
  - Wing 103
- Training Wing, Cambridge University ... 47
- Volunteer Reserve 47, 67, 71

Royal Australian Air Force 63
Royal Canadian Air Force 106

Schools
- Brighton, Brighton College 73
- Burbage
  - National, Church of England 25, 29, 34, 47, 56, 67, 71, 89, 92
  - Secondary School, Grove Road ... 25, 47
  - Wesleyan Day 51, 112, 117
- Hinckley, Grammar School 66, 71

Sports
- Baseball 109, 112
- Cricket 32
- Football 29
- Rugby Football 32, 47, 67

Topics
- Air Cadets 105
- Army Reserves 83
- Atomic Bombs 134
- Axis Forces 54
- Bicycle Infantry 63
- Blackouts 124
- British Fourteenth Army 96
- Burbage Parish Council 104
- Burbage Spitfire Appeal 131
- Darky Call System (RAF) 103
- First World War 9, 10, 63, 75, 81, 116, 125
- Italian Armistice 18
- Italian Invasion 18, 58, 79
- Leicester War Memorials at Risk Project 123
- Leicestershire, Lord Lieutenant of ... 12
- Name Changes, Countries 9
- Poem For Johnny 105
- Red Cross 67
- Remembrance Sunday 27
- Rolls Royce 81

Rolls Royce Merlin	50
School Engagement	8
Scout Movement	47
Scripture Readings	13
Territorial Army	34
Tutankhamen	60
Waziristan Campaign, Afghanistan	63
WW2	9

Towns, Villages & Locations
- Bedfordshire, Luton 100
- Birmingham, Queen Elizabeth Hospital 73
- Canadian Embassy 105
- Coventry & Warwickshire Hospital 81
- Lancashire, New Brighton 34
- Leicester Grange, Wolvey 115
- Leicestershire
  - Aston Flamville 71
  - Dunton Bassett 33
  - Leicester 73
  - Lutterworth, Misterton Hall 12
  - Smockington 18
- Lincolnshire
  - Grantham 75
  - Lincoln 83
  - Sleaford 71
- Merioneth, Transfynydd 100
- Norfolk 100
- Northamptonshire, Towcester 61
- Norwich, City of, Aviation Museum, ... 50
- Nottinghamshire
  - Calverton 94
  - Nottingham 75
- Nuneaton Mining School 47
- Roxburghshire, Hawick 100
- Staffordshire, Wolverhampton 26
- University of Oxford, Balliol College 116
- Warwickshire
  - Bulkington, Ryton 51
  - Coventry 79, 89
  - Nuneaton 18
  - Stockingford 39
  - Wolvey 18, 41
- Wisbech, Fenland Aviation Mus. & Aircraft Preserv. 50
- Worcestershire
  - Hall Green 60
  - Moseley 60
- Yorkshire, Scarborough 75

War Cemeteries
- Algeria, Dely Ibrahim 54
- Austria, Klagenfurt 89
- France
  - Calvados, La Delivrande 21
  - Chartres, St Cheron 52
  - St. Desir, Calvados 51, 52
- Germany, Berlin 1939-1945 67
- Italy
  - Beach Head, Anzio 18, 58
  - Coriano Ridge 79
  - Gradara 29
- Netherlands
  - Gelderland, Canadian 23
  - Osterbeek 56
- Poland, Malbork 25, 26
- Thailand
  - Akyab 42
  - Chungkai 92, 102
  - Kanchanaburi 37, 63, 102
  - Mandalay 42
  - Meiktila 42
  - Sahmaw 42
  - Taukkyan, Myanmar 41, 42, 96, 102
- Tunisia
  - Enfidaville 44, 87
  - Massicault 27
  - Sfax 34, 35

War Memorials
- Bullkington, St James' Church 51
- Burbage
  - Congregational Chapel 21, 27, 29, 37, 92
  - Liberal Club 29, 34, 75
  - Plaque, Sgt John Howarth, St Catherine's Church 47
  - Plaque, WO John Lord, St Catherine's Church 67
  - Rose Garden 10
  - St Catherine's Church 18, 21, 23, 25, 27, 29, 32, 34, 39, 41, 44, 47, 51, 54, 56, 58, 60, 66, 67, 73, 75, 79, 81, 87, 92, 94
  - The Memorial 11, 16, 18, 21, 23, 25, 27, 29, 32, 34, 37, 39, 41, 44, 47, 51, 54, 56, 58, 60, 63, 66, 67, 73, 75, 79, 81, 83, 84, 87, 89, 92, 94, 96, 97
  - Unveiling 13, 14
  - Wesleyan Chapel 44, 51, 96, 97
- Burma
  - Rangoon 42, 83, 84
  - Taukkyan 42
- Chatham, Naval 39, 40
- Coventry, Civilian Memorial, London Road Cemetery 81
- Dunton Bassett 32
- France, Normandy 52
- Hinckley
  - Grammar School 71, 87, 120
  - Holy Trinity Church 34, 35, 66
  - Regent Club 27, 66
  - The Memorial 27, 54
- India, Bhowanipore, Calcutta 94
- Netherlands, Groesbeek 23, 24